Asterian Astrology is revolutionary and will change the way we view Astrology forever.
Shri Ananda Das-*Hinduism Today*

Jade Luna has been amazing in assisting me in my career and my personal life.
Courteney Cox-*Cougar Town, Friends*

I love Jade Luna's readings. He is the most pinpoint accurate astrologer out there. His system and guidance have been invaluable.
Rashida Jones, *I Love You, Man, Parks & Recreation*

Jade Luna's wisdom and knowledge are matched perfectly with his heart and compassion. I am deeply grateful for his astrological guidance on my path.
Sheryl Lee, *Twin Peaks*

Jade Luna's system of astrology and his readings were extremely beneficial for me, giving me great insight and guidance.
Drena De Niro

Jade Luna's insight and understanding of the truth of astrology is outstanding. It has served me and stands to serve us all.
Regina Hall, Actress, *Scary Movie, Death at a Funeral & Ally McBeal.*

Jade Luna is a masterful Astrologer.
Terence Trent D'Arby, *singer -songwriter, Wishing Well*

Asterian Astrology is a gem 2,300 years in the making.
Franl Lanz, *Yogaltaliono Magazine*

TARA INTERNATIONAL

INDIA RESEARCH PRESS / TARA PRESS INTERNATIONAL

INDIA

Corporate Office -
B-4/22,Khajuraho - 110 029, INDIA
Telephone :   91-11-2369 4610 Telefax :   91-11-2471 8637

Editorial Office -

Flat #6, TRUST OFFICE - 110003, India.
Tel: 00.91.11.2469 4610, 2469 4855
TeleFAX: 00.91.11.24618637, 417 57 113

AMERICA

JSL INC Press.
14431 Ventura Blvd suite 538
Sherman Oaks CA 91423
www.asterianastrology.com

This book was edited in India and editorial errors may exist.

Dedicated to Gianna for her Love and Hecate for being the
origin of it all

ASTERIAN ASTROLOGY VOL. I ™

(The Lost System of Alexander the Great)

"The Yavanas (Greeks) are warriors (Barbarians), yet the science of astronomy originated with them and for this they must be reverenced like gods."
The Gargi-Samhita (Vedic Astrology Text)

FORWARD:
(a transition from West to East and back to West again).

I met Jade Sol Luna in early 2003 - the way most people do – over the phone. After hearing about the Vedic astrologer from mutual friends for four years, I had finally decided to schedule a reading. Although I was entirely skeptical, as an attorney I believed myself to be skilled at using logic and reason to navigate my own success, I was curious and looking forward to being entertained. A close friend of mine had been telling me about Jade, who not only was able to relay specific details about her career and fittingly described her relationships and interactions with her boyfriend and loved ones, but also enlightened her to upcoming world trends that have all came to pass, as well as personal events in her own life. What was most impressive was that he did so without asking for the slightest information about my friend – all she said was "hello" over the phone and then sat silently for the next forty minutes as he told her shockingly accurate details about her life.

My first reading, which was of my Vedic   birth chart, was nearly the same experience. After saying "hello," I sat on the phone in silence for thirty minutes as he spoke in a clear, articulate voice about me. He knew things that I have never revealed to my most intimate friends or even a drunken stranger. What further fascinated me was that he predicted some upcoming trends for the year that actually came to pass, if not on the date, then right before it. Looking back on that first reading, I now realize that if I had prepared for some of the trends Jade predicted, mainly those personalities, concerns, and desires of people with whom I would have close contact, I would have made smarter, healthier, and more beneficial choices for me. Instead, I continued to do things my own way. Finally, after three years of his incredibly informative readings – still having never met the man – I finally started to heed his advice. My life has never been more fulfilling, more satisfying, and more abundant.

When I met Jade, he was just coming out of his tenure as a Brahmin priest. As I was just beginning my own studies in meditation and chanting in Sanskrit, his readings helped me to further understand Eastern philosophy, making the ancient teachings relatable to a modern LA woman living and working in the heart of New York City. During my readings, he was honest and forthcoming in his explanations of the practical applications of Vedic astrology as they pertained to my life. Jade truly has a remarkable skill for applying Eastern beliefs to Western living, a gift (I believe) stemming from his successful career in the music industry living in Los Angeles and later his years spent as a Brahmin priest. How often does a city man completely turn within, become a Brahmin, and immerse himself in ancient Eastern spiritual teachings?

Jade's readings are informative, practical, and user-friendly, taking the time to interpret even the most complicated astrological charts in a way that his listener might understand. During personal readings, he dissects the astrological information so that his clients can begin to apply the knowledge to their own lives. His understanding of the detailed minutiae of Vedic astrology is vast and yet personal, as he is skilled in translating the pertinent astrological information to anyone in the West.

In particular, Jade is a teacher and leader in the field of educating people in the West about their "shadow" side. Never hurtful, he illuminates his students to their shadows unearthed by the astrology report to help them recognize that without contrast, one can never fully appreciate the light. His efforts are focused on each client's ability to experience his or her own true sense of being a part of the fabric of all life and connecting to others with a true sense of love and appreciation for the bigger picture. My own friends have even said that at first, Jade's willingness to look at the shadowy places within them was intimidating, but each one of them was incredibly grateful to recognize his or her own shadowy characteristics as valid and a necessary link for detaching from the mundane.

In Jade's new book, he has shown me, and many others, the reverse side of his personal studies. Not only has he presented a method of Vedic astrology interpretation that is reliable and personal, but he has also introduced detailed comparisons of Hindu and Indian symbols, Gods, Goddesses, philosophies and meditation to Greek, Celtic and other ancient philosophies and religions. Jade's passion to fuse all of the teachings across our planet, as well as to help us all make sense of various spiritual traditions is what this book offers to anyone desiring to deeply know himself or herself.

It is my hope that you will read Jade's book with an open mind and heart. Truly a friend to all, Jade wants each of his students to feel fulfilled and live to her or his own potential by embracing oneself for who one is – both light and dark. From that exalted place of inner knowing, his students can make great choices in their own lives.

Jade Luna and The Modern Dilemma (2012)

31% of Americans believe in astrology so you can understand why people got hysterical in January, 2011 when Parke Kunkle, a Minnesota astronomer, confirmed what many (including Jade Luna, Vedic Astrologers and Sidereal Astrologers) have believed for years: the way the Earth has shifted on its axis over the past 3,000 years has changed the 12 zodiac signs. This is called the precession of the equinox or more commonly, "the wobble," and what it means is that **you may not be the sign you think you are**.

Asterian Astrology will provide readers with an astronomically correct form of astrology that they can depend on to understand themselves and those people in their lives that compel and confound them. This information is controversial but change always is. Remember when everyone believed that the earth was flat (not!)? Or that smoking was actually good for you (insert cough sound and cloudy chest x-ray)? Or that yoga was only for hippies (now a 57 billion dollar industry). The truth is a hard pill to swallow.

Despite the fact that the precession of the equinox and how it affects astrological signs can be proven by astronomy, astrology followers are not completely convinced. You see, they've gotten attached to their sign and the identity that it represents. Geminis like having an alibi for their "split personalities." Cancers like having a good excuse for why they want to stay at home all the time. And Sagittarians want a justification for why they keep putting their foot in their mouths embarrassing themselves and others with TMI. Yet, a gnawing feeling has those same followers reading the sign that comes before theirs just to be sure.

finding out that the person one believed was their father isn't actually their father. It'd be shocking at first. There'd be a lot of questions. Doubts. Fears. But overtime, who wouldn't want to know their real parent and all the things that person might reveal about them.

With great respect, **Barbie Baylis -** Entertainment Lawyer for Pearl Jam, Attorney-At-Law, Business Manager of The Hub yoga studio in West Los Angeles

THE ORIGIN OF ASTROLOGY

"Astrology developed in India in stages. The earliest stage was of native ideas about the stars and the future, found primarily in the Vedas. Mesopotamian astral omens also became known, perhaps during the Achaemenian period. But Greek astrology came to India during the first century CE, from Alexandria, and was adopted enthusiastically. Most astrology in India today is Greek astrology. But it is Greek astrology heavily modified to fit Indian society. As a result, it is in modern India that classical astrology, including astral religion, is most alive and powerful. The modern Euro-American revival of belief in astrology is due in part to the Theosophical Society's promotion of Indian astrology."
-From Sphudjidhvaja in "The Yavanajataka"

*The **Yavanajataka-** (Sanskrit for "Saying (Jataka) of the Greeks (Yavanas)") is the earliest writing of Indian astrology. It is a translation from Greek to Sanskrit made by "Yavanesvara" ("Lord of the Greeks") in 149–150 CE, under the rule of the Western Kshatrapa king Rudrakarman I, and then versified 120 years later by Sphujidhwaja.*

The original Greek text is considered to have been written around 120 BCE in Alexandria. It is India's earliest Sanskrit work in horoscopy, followed by other works of Western origin which greatly influenced Indian astrology: the Paulisa Siddhanta ("Doctrine of Paul"), and the Romaka Siddhanta ("Doctrine of the Romans").

There is general agreement that a rudimentary astrological system was developed in Mesopotamia in the 2nd or 3rd millennium BCE. However, unlike astrology as we know and use it today, these ancient Mesopotamians, in particular the ancient Babylonian priests, used astrology to know the "divine" will of their gods and to communicate it to their kings. Astrology's function related to the affairs of the nation, not to its individuals. The priests, known as "inspectors," would observe – or inspect – the Sun, Moon, stars and planets. They began to record celestial events and to connect them with contemporaneous earthly events – wars, famines, floods, and so on. By the 7th century BCE, as their knowledge of astronomy expanded, the Babylonians' simple astrological system evolved into a more complex system. Because they were now able to predict astronomical events based on their growing astronomical knowledge, the Babylonian priests were able to use the information that they had recorded through the centuries to predict and interpret future events. There is evidence to suggest that during this period Babylonians were interested in the use of astrology by individuals, at least to the point of developing an individual's horoscope at the time of birth. They identified patterns of stars in the night sky and named what we now call constellations. These constellations came to be symbolized in a 12-sign zodiac. This Babylonian system and zodiac evolved to become the Tropical astrology used by Western astrologers today. *Although the book *Ancient Astronomy and Celestial Divination* by Swerdlow has insurmountable evidence that the Babylonians observed precession.

And then came Alexander. While the Greeks had a powerful tie with Egyptian astrology, it was not until Alexander the Great's conquests in Mesopotamia in the late 4th century BCE that the Greeks came into direct contact with the

Mesopotamian systems of astrology, corrected them and transformed them, and then expanded them into one coherent system. Through Alexander's conquest into northern India, this Hellenistic astrology was introduced to India and influenced the development of Hindu (Vedic) astrology.

The word "astrology" itself is Greek and means "science of the stars," and the Greeks are credited by some with creating the foundation for modern astrology. Alexander himself was known to have consulted with astrologers. Astrology flourished during the Hellenistic period, benefiting from the exchange ideas by the newly united cultures. Nowhere was this more evident than in Alexander's own city of Alexandria. Alexandria was an intellectual center of thought and philosophy, if not the intellectual center, of the Hellenistic world. The Greeks during the Hellenistic period created a horoscope based on the position of the planets and the stars when a person is born which would in turn determine personal traits of that individual. This is called natal astrology and was one of three key features of Hellenistic astrology, the others being universal (prediction of events) and katarchic (selection of propitious times for activities). They also developed the concept of "houses" in which the "signs" of the zodiac (a Greek word meaning "circle of animals") reside.

In 130 BCE, the Greek astronomer Hipparchus developed the theory of precession which was to have a great impact on the studies of astronomy and non-Western astrology. The Hellenistic astrologer and astronomer Ptolemy (85-165 CE) wrote Tetrabiblos, a treatise on astrology that is considered by some to be a basis of Western astrology. Ptolemy ignored the discoveries of Hipparchus.

Rome

Initially, in the 1st century BCE during the Roman Republic, upper class Romans discouraged the practice of astrology, dismissing it as superstition. However, Romans admired Greek culture, and eventually Romans grew interested in and incorporated Hellenistic astrology into their own belief systems. In the 1st century CE, Marcus Manilius wrote the *Astronomica*, a poem in five books which he dedicated to Caesar Augustus. Among other astrological concepts, Manilius believed the Moon sign took priority in a birth chart. It is extremely important to note that the Moon sign, was extremely important, if not primary, in both Hellenistic and Roman astrology. The Moon was first in importance, the Sun was second and the rising sign was third. Astrology became part of everyday life in ancient Rome. Augustus had coins minted with his profile on one side and his Moon sign, on the other. Augustus publicly used astrology and recognized its power enough to restrict it. Two things were made illegal during his reign: astrological consultations without witnesses and astrological consultations about death.

India

As noted earlier, Hellenistic astrology was introduced to India by Alexander the Great and influenced the development of Hindu astrology. Unlike Tropical astrology, Jyotish is not oriented to the Sun, but rather to the actual positions of the constellations. This means it incorporates the concept of precession. In India, the precession of the equinox is called *the ayanamsha*.

To Hellenistic astrology (that is, the lunar astrology of the Greeks and Romans), Hindu astrologers superimposed their concept of the nakshatras, the 27 Stars in which the Moon signs reside. They also oriented their zodiac to the actual positions of the constellations. Throughout the centuries, Hindu astrology has continued to give precedence to Moon signs over Sun signs and have incorporated the astronomical concept of precession. Greek, Roman, and Hindu astrologers shared in the belief of the primacy of Stars. The Moon in these belief systems was thought to be an indicator of a person's personality – his or her psyche. Greek and Roman astrology virtually disappeared during the disintegration of the Mother Goddess in the Western Roman Empire. The surviving system – Hindu astrology – continues that tradition. Astrology has survived from our very earliest history as we, and those who came before us, have struggled to make sense of and find meaning in our lives.

Astronomy versus Astrology

When astronomy and astrology were developed, they were related disciplines often performed by the same person who first "inspected" the skies and then interpreted his observations. During the "Age of Enlightenment," that relationship was finally severed, as one discipline was labeled "science" and the other "divination." However, one of the most important astronomical discoveries – that of precession of the equinoxes – had a profound effect on the development of various astrological systems.

Ancient Disciplines

Ancient people looked up at the night sky and must have felt the same sense of wonder that many of us feel today. The evidence of their wonder is their work in attempting to understand this wondrous sky through astronomy and astrology. With astronomy, they focused on the physical knowledge of the objects now called constellations and planets.

With astrology, ancient people tried to understand the metaphysical influences these beautiful physical objects exerted in their own lives. Underlying both disciplines was the belief that our world is somehow divinely ordered. In the beginning, astronomy and astrology were considered legitimate and related scientific studies. In fact, in ancient times, the astronomer and the astrologer were often the same person, typically a priest. During the Christian era, this began to change with the anti-divination laws enacted through the influence of the early church. However, it was only during the 18th century that the two areas of study were viewed as two completely separate disciplines. One was now considered science and the other strictly divination. But many astrological principles of Hindu astrology in particular are based on astronomical concepts.

The Ecliptic

The ecliptic – or the position of the Sun as it is perceived from the revolving earth –seems to pass through the constellations that form the Tropical, or Western, zodiac (Aries, Taurus, Gemini, Cancer, Leo, Virgo, Libra, Scorpio, Sagittarius,

Capricorn, Aquarius and Pisces), even though it is actually passing in front of these constellations. A person's zodiac Sun sign is determined by the constellation through which the Sun was "passing through" on the day he or she was born. Early astronomers observed the Sun traveling through the signs of the zodiac in the course of one year, spending about one month in each. Thus, they calculated that each constellation extends 30 degrees across the ecliptic. However, a phenomenon called precession of the equinoxes has altered and continues to alter the position of the constellations.

Precession (directional change) of the equinoxes

In 130 CE, Hipparchus discovered the concept of precession of the equinoxes (although there is evidence that the Egyptians were aware of precession). Precession results from gravitational forces of the Sun, Moon, planets, etc., causing a very slow movement of the earth's axis in the shape of a circle. Imagine a "pole" extending from the north and south equinoxes (or poles). Now imagine that pole moving around the bottom of a cone. The entire cycle around the bottom of the cone takes between 23,000 and 26,000 years. This is precession of the equinoxes. Therefore the constellations we see today are not the constellations ancient people saw – even if they were standing on the same spot at the same date and time of day in the year as we are.

Astrology is based for the most part on the position of the Sun in relation to the constellations. It is concerned with energy of a magnitude that is difficult to conceptualize. Our planet moves, creating energy, in three ways: (i) it revolves, creating night and day; (ii) it orbits the Sun creating the seasons; and

(iii) it precedes. Precession is the slow gyration of our planet's axis.

Astrology is an individual's own weather forecast and, depending upon the alignments (weather patterns) that one experiences, these vast energies provide an awareness which can directly affect the choices that person will make and how those choices can impact his or her daily life.

Tropical

Today Tropical astrology is the primary system of astrology used in the West. It is the source for the zodiac calendar familiar to most of us. The problem is that Tropical astrology is flawed. It is flawed because it does not include the astronomical concept of precession. As a result, the Tropical zodiac is not aligned with the actual positions of the constellations, and it fails to exactly align with the seasons. Even worse, Tropical astrology erroneously applies northern hemisphere seasons to the whole planet when in fact the large populations in the southern hemisphere experience the seasons and alignment with the constellations six months apart from those in the northern hemisphere. Tropical astrology of today is 23 degrees off the star constellations so central to it.

The Problem with Tropical

As mentioned multiple times, Tropical astrology is the primary system used today by Western astrologers. It is ancient and, like the other systems, is based on the astrological work of the Mesopotamians. Unlike the other systems, it has not technically advanced to the extent of the others. It does not incorporate, for example, the astronomical concept of precession of the equinoxes. As a result, there is no direct relationship between it and the ecliptic (that is, the placement of the Sun with relation to the constellations – at the time, day, and location of one's birth). In other words, it is not a flexible system based on astronomical phenomenon. Because of this inflexibility, it uses a 12-sign zodiac whose signs do not relate to the actual constellations today. They only symbolize those constellations. The signs are actually based on the position of the Sun at the time the Tropical zodiac was originally created, 4 to 5 millennia ago.

Sidereal

Sidereal is also an ancient system and has been used by Indian astrologers for thousands of years. It also was influenced by certain aspects of Mesopotamian astrology. Sidereal astrology, however, does incorporate the concept of precession. As a result, it is based on the actual positions of the constellations. Unlike Tropical astrology, Sidereal is a precession based system. Sidereal shares with Tropical astrology a 12-sign zodiac. When the Tropical and Sidereal zodiacs were developed in approximately 1,900 BCE, both were based on what was observed in the sky at that time. Because of the Sidereal system's inclusion of precession, however, the Sidereal zodiac is dynamic, and the two zodiacs are no longer in sync. Modern Astronomers agree that the difference in the ecliptic between the two zodiacs is now approximately 23 degrees.

Hellenistic

During the conquests of Alexander the Great, the Greeks came into direct contact with the Mesopotamian systems of astrology. They embraced, developed, and "codified" them into a highly organized system. Many of the astrological concepts we are familiar with today were creations of the Greeks (for example, the use of one's horoscope as a predictive tool in everyday life). When Alexander conquered the northern areas of India, the Hindus adopted the Hellenistic system.

The Romans were influenced as well, particularly during the early to mid-Roman Empire. It has been suggested that the Romans in fact wholly adopted the astrology of the Greeks, adding Romanized names for the various constellations and planets. However, not much is known today about the astrological system of the Romans – most likely as a result of the anti-divination campaign during the final days of the Western Roman Empire.

Jyotish

Evidence of the powerful influence of Hellenistic astrology on Hindu astrology is documented in The Yavanajataka, the Sanskrit translation of an original Greek text from Alexandria that is the basis of today's Hindu astrology (Jyotish). Hindu astrology, like Greco-Roman, is lunar-based. It consists of 27 Stars (nakshatras) and incorporates the concept of precession. As a result, like Sidereal, its zodiac is a dynamic reflection of the stellar positions at the time of one's birth. Because of its incorporation of the astronomical concept of precession and because it uses 27 signs instead of the 12-sign Tropical or Sidereal systems, Hindu astrology has a more precise focus. Hindu astrology is a highly accurate though not necessarily accessible system of astrology. My primary interest in Hindu astrology is that it provides a path back to Alexander's system as developed by the Greeks and adopted by the Romans, through its foundational document The Yavanajataka.

Why the name Asterian Astrology?

My focus as an astrologer has been to re-create the Greco-Roman system. I call this recreation Asterian Astrology due to the fact that Alexander the Great's priests channeled the Goddess Asteria (Hecate's Mother) for all Astrological insight. Asteria was the stars (Stars) and her daughter Hecate was the Moon that traveled through them.

The Stars

In the Asterian astrological system, there are 27 Lunar Stars that divide the sky. The Stars provide the structure of Asterian Astrology. These conceptually relate to the signs of the Tropical zodiac, 2.33 consecutive Stars are roughly equivalent to one zodiac sign. This gives the Asterian Astrology system far greater exactitude than the Tropical system. Each Star is identified by the prominent cluster of stars in and around each of the constellations. The Sun passes through the 27 lunar Stars during its annual cycle.

Each Star is named for the "ruling" Roman/Greco god or goddess (also called angel) through whose constellation the

Moon traveled – for approximately one day – during its monthly cycle. The God or Goddess that rules over the position of the Sun is also observed. These gods/Stars can be divided into three categories, or natures: angelic, human, and infernal. To the ancient Romans, these categories represented the three natures of God.

Sun versus Moon

In the Asterian system of astrology, the Moon takes priority over the Sun. Scientifically, the Moon controls the tides on this planet, and humans are somewhere between seventy to ninety percent water. The Sun defines the power of a person, but the Moon defines the nature, personality, and the sub-conscious of a person. The Sun is our conscious mind and the Moon is the sub-conscious mind. **In modern time, we act more from our sub-conscious then our conscious mind, hence the Moon takes priority over the Sun. The Sun represents our power, authority and the thoughts stored in the Divine Mind but the Moon represents the thoughts that turn to actions.**

Image of the Precession

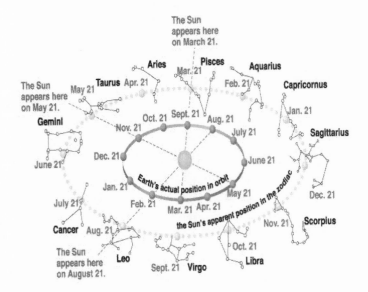

As this picture clearly illustrates, on March 21st, Spring equinox is 7 degrees Pisces not 1 degrees of Aries. The precession of the Equinox was observed by the, Buddhists, Hindus and mastered by the Greeks. It was Hipparchus and the Priests of Alexander that were responsible for mastering the calculations of the Equinox. In the Yavanajataka, Alexander calls the tropical Western system of Astrology "for the uneducated". Tropical Astrology is the ONLY system that fails to calculate the precession making it false. This is not an opinion, but a fact. Call your local Astronomer and he will tell you the same thing.

ASTERIAN ASTROLOGY

Asterian Astrology and the Moon

The **Moon** is the earth's companion satellite, though some astronomers believe that it approaches being a planet in its own right. The Moon is large enough for its gravity to affect the Earth, stabilizing its orbit and producing the regular ebb and flow of the tides. The Moon is also familiar to us for its different phases, waxing and waning in appearance in an unchanging cycle.

The Moon orbits the earth in 28 days, spending a fleeting 2.33 days in each of the Signs of the zodiac. Recently, more accurate measurements of the Lunar orbital period have revealed two different numbers, depending on viewpoint. The synodic period is measured relative to the Sun and gives us a period of 29.5 days from new Moon to new Moon, the start of the lunar month. When observed from the earth and relative to a fixed point in space, the sidereal period is 27.3 days with minor variations. In order to give a figure in whole numbers for ease of astrological calculation the Lunar orbit can be approximated to 27.75 days which then returns a period of 54 hours or 2.25 days for the Lunar transit of each Sign.

The Moon is the most important planet in a person's birth chart, thus Asterian Astrology is observed by the Moon first and Sun second. In the greatest sense, the Moon is the concept of nature on all levels as what nurtures, sustains, protects, and yet is always changing; we say Mother Nature. The Lunar cycle correlates with the menstrual cycle of women, influences the tides of the oceans, and can be very important in agriculture as when to plant and when to reap. The Moon controls the tides on this planet and human beings are 70% water, therefore the

Moon describes the nature of the basic self. The Moon as the Earth's satellite, symbolizes the reflection of the soul in and around the body. In a general sense this is the psychic material world, more specifically the Moon represents the personality, feelings, moods, habits, memory, impressionability, imagination, emotions, and the subconscious. The subconscious stores all your karma and impressions from previous lives. Lunar Astrology assists in helping a person become aware of their subconscious, thus speeding up the process of self awareness.

The Moon is a prevalent symbol for every human being on this planet. In ancient times writers referred to the soul as feminine and symbolized by the Moon. All beings come from the same place, a mother's womb. The first part of life in the womb and as a baby relate to the Moon, because the mother is the dominant influence during this period. This is also significant for the development of the basic self which will remember everything the conscious self forgets. Asterian Astrology then becomes important because the Moon continually fluctuates as it waxes from new Moon to full Moon and wanes down to a new Moon again. Every being on the planet is directly affected by this process.

The Sun, Mercury, Venus, and Mars usually change Signs only about once a month, and the outer planets in periods of years. But the Moon traverses the zodiac in 27.3 days. So the day-to-day interpretations are usually based primarily on changes of the Moon Sign and the Lunar Mansion. It is interesting to note that the astrology columns which usually appear in daily papers for the Sun Signs are often based primarily on the position of the Moon.

The full Moon tends to bring out extremes of the basic self in eating, drinking, emotions, desires, etc. Thus the word lunacy came from Luna, or Moon. In ancient culture they worshipped the Moon more than the Sun.

In the world of astrology, the Sun symbolizes the light body. Of course the light body is transcendent of the distinction between male and female, and the symbolism of the Sun or Moon. However, these concepts have been used to point to the higher truth that is beyond conception, but just is.

STARS (LUNAR MANSIONS)

There are 27 Star (Lunar Mansion) divisions of the sky, identified by a prominent cluster of stars in and around the constellations. The Moon passes through them during its monthly cycle, as used in ancient astronomy and astrology. Therefore, each Star represents a division of the ecliptic similar to the zodiac (13°20 each instead of the 30° for each zodiac Sign, although Prometheus and Vulcan are a little smaller). The orbit of the Moon is 27.3 days, so the Moon takes approximately one day to pass through each Star.

The starting point for a Star is the place on the ecliptic directly opposite of the star Spica (other slightly different definitions exist). It is called the "Start of Aries". The ecliptic is divided into each of the Stars eastward.

Each Star is governed as 'Lord' by one of the nine main planets in the following sequence: South Node, Venus, Sun, Moon, Mars, North Node, Jupiter, Saturn and Mercury. This cycle repeats itself three times to cover all 27 Lunar Mansions/Stars; this book reveals each of the 27 Stars and their meanings, with their equivalent positions in the Sidereal Zodiac.

In astrology the Stars are a division of the ecliptic similar to the Zodiac. The mansion associated with a given date corresponds to a portion of the constellation wherein the Moon is passing through at that time. In Asterian Astrology, there are 27 Stars, covering 13°20 degrees of the ecliptic.

The Sun, the Secondary Presence of Asterian Astrology

(The REAL Constellations of the Zodiac)

The ecliptic, or the position of the Sun as it's perceived from the revolving Earth, passes through the constellations which form the Zodiac: Aries, Taurus, Gemini, Cancer, Leo, Virgo, Libra, Scorpio, Sagittarius, Capricorn, Aquarius and Pisces. Zodiac Signs were originally determined by which constellation the Sun was "in" on the day you were born.

Early astronomers observed the Sun traveling through the Signs of the Zodiac in the course of one year, spending about a month in each. Thus, they calculated each constellation extends 30 degrees across the ecliptic.

However, a phenomenon called precession has altered the position of the constellations we see today.

More Understanding of Precession and Astrology

The first day of spring in the Northern Hemisphere was once marked by the zero point of the Zodiac. Astronomers call this the vernal equinox and it occurs as the ecliptic and celestial equator intersect.

Around 600 BCE, the zero point was in Aries and was called the "first point of Aries." The constellation Aries encompassed the first 30 degrees of the ecliptic; from 30 to 60 degrees was Taurus; from 60 to 90 degrees was Gemini; and so on for all twelve constellations of the Zodiac.

The Earth continually wobbles around its axis in a 25,800-year cycle. This wobble, called precession, is caused by the gravitational attraction of the Moon on Earth's equatorial bulge.

Over the past two-and-a-half millennia, this wobble has caused the intersection point between the celestial equator and the ecliptic to move west along the ecliptic by 36 degrees, or almost exactly one-tenth of the way around. This means that the Signs have slipped one-tenth, or almost one whole month, of the way around the sky to the west, relative to the stars beyond.

For instance, those born between March 21 and April 19 consider themselves to be Aries. Today, the Sun is no longer within the constellation of Aries during much of that period. From March 13 to April 13, the Sun is actually in the constellation of Pisces, which demonstrates the precession of the equinoxes from 600 BCE to 2600.

Your "Real Sun Sign"

The table below lists the dates when the Sun is actually within the astronomical constellations of the Zodiac, according to modern constellation boundaries and corrected for precession (these dates can vary a day from year to year).

Check out your "real" zodiac Sign and see what the sky looked like on your birthday.

Capricorn - Jan 13 to Feb 14

Aquarius - Feb 14 to Mar 13

Pisces - Mar 13 to Apr 13

Aries - Apr 13 to May 14

Taurus - May 14 to Jun 14

Gemini - Jun 14 to Jul 15

Cancer - Jul 15 to Aug 16

Leo - Aug 16 to Sep 16

Virgo - Sep 16 to Oct 16

Libra - Oct 16 to Nov 15

Scorpio - Nov 16 to Dec 15

Sagittarius - Dec15 to Jan 13

Before you start to analyze your Sun Sign take note of the Star it falls under (dates listed under Star Chapter page 52). The Star is the main essence of a person and the Sun Sign colors the Star.

The Play of the Sun and Moon

Where the Moon plays the stronger role of your earthly expression, the Sun plays the role of the spiritual force that drives that expression. The play of the Moon and the Sun together reveal the true nature of an individual. Look to the

Moon to see how a person will express themselves, but the Suns placement will show the force that drives the earthly expression (having a thought does not mean that you will take action on that thought, the Moon determines which thoughts turn into actions).

Every living human has three bodies: the gross body (the physical body), the subtle body (the power or energy body) and the mental body (the thought or light body).

The physical body is the body we see and use for earthly experiences, it is ruled over in Astrology by the rising Sign. The subtle body is connected to one's personal power and emotional expression, and is ruled over by the Moon. The Sun is connected to the mental body and radiates a person's individual thought process. Thoughts manifest from the Sun (mental body) and are expressed through the Moon (power body) as emotions. The physical body (rising Sign) is created from your mental and power bodies. The Moon is the most significant of the three because the power body has the greatest impact on the way we feel and act. It is true that the Sun is the guiding force of Astrology, but because we are human beings and prediction is the essence of most Astrology, the Moon plays the most significant role.

In ancient Roman Astrology the Moon is the most important planet. This is because it represents all emotions which in turn create physical action. The spirit (Moon or Luna) takes the light of the soul (Sun or Sol) and reflects it into manifested creation. It differentiates the light of the Sun through waxing and waning. Consequently, the Sign and especially the Star that the Moon falls within, will have an enormous bearing on the personality of an individual. The Moon's relationship to the other planets reflects a person's attitude and whether they have or lack stability and if they are conscious of change. I like to use the words "stability or change" instead of "success or failure" because in the ancient world, change was often equated with failure. In those times it wasn't common for an individual to decide to pick up and move across the country, change careers and start over. Cultural and economic conditions prevented these events from taking place. So, more often than not, the person going through major changes would face ruination. Please keep in mind that in modern times, the more difficult Stars of the Moon are related to change and obstacles. Destruction and ruination must be seen from all aspects of the horoscope.

THE ROMAN CALENDAR

The Origin/Name of the Months

January - Janus, Roman God of doors and beginnings, Sunset and Sunrise, had one face looking forward and one backward.

February - On February 15th -16th the Romans celebrated the festival of forgiveness for sins; (in Latin: februare, to purify). This was also the evening that the Sun moved into Aquarius and this constellation was equated with sinful actions. Neptune's home is Aegeon and is in the center of Aquarius.

March - The Roman God of war, Mars, rules over this month.

April - In Rome this month is Aprilis, perhaps derived from the Latin word: aperire, to open, as in opening buds and blossoms; or perhaps from Aphrodite, original Greek name of Venus.

May - Maia, a Roman Goddess, mother of Mercury and daughter of Atlas, rules over this month.

June - Juno, the chief Roman Goddess, rules over this month.

July - Renamed after Julius Caesar, born this month in 44 BC (in Latin: quintilis, meaning 5 was the former name). The Roman year began in March rather than January.

August - Formerly named Sextilis (sixth month in the Roman calendar); re-named in 8 BC for Augustus Caesar.

September - The seventh month in the Julian or Roman calendar (in Latin: Septem, meaning 7), established in the reign of Julius Caesar.

October - The eighth month in the Julian or Roman calendar (in Latin: Octo, meaning 8). The Gregorian calendar instituted by Pope Gregory XIII established January as the first month of the year.

November - The ninth month in the Roman calendar (in Latin: novem, meaning 9). Catholic countries adopted the Gregorian calendar in 1582, skipping 10 days that October, correcting for too many leap years. November 16th is the celebration of the Goddess Hecate as the Sun spends his first full day in the constellation Scorpio (home of the Goddess Hecate).

December -The tenth month in the Julian or Roman calendar (in Latin: decem, meaning 10).

The Days of the Week

"The custom, however, of referring the days to the seven stars called planets was instituted by the Egyptians, but is now found among all mankind." (Cassius Dio, History of Rome, XXXVII, 18.1)

The astrological or planetary week of seven days is thought to have started in Persian theology, and by the end of the first century AD was in common usage throughout the whole Mediterranean world. Although the planetary week was recognized by Emperor Augustus, he continued to run the ancient calendar alongside it. Then in 321 AD, during the rule of Emperor Constantine, the astrological week became fully established in Roman law. Later in history, Catholicism was responsible for changing the names. Monday used to be called Moonday; they took the "N" out of Saturday as it used to be called Saturnday. The seven days used to be the seven main personalities of God, but based upon modern dualism, God is now only seen as one aspect as the Sun, hence the name Sunday was untouched.

The Astrological Week

Roman- Translation-Equivalent-Derivation

SATURDAY-dies Saturni' the day of Saturn' Saturday. From Latin descent.

SUNDAY- Solis' Sun day' Sunday. From Latin descent.

MONDAY- Lunae'Moon day' Monday. From Latin descent.

TUESDAY- dies Martis' the day of Mars. 'Tuesday *Tiwesdaeg* 'the day of Tiw', from Norse *Tysdagrdies*

WEDNESDAY- Mercuris' the day of Mercury'. Wednesday *Wodnesdaeg* 'the day of Woden'

THURSDAY- from Norse *Odins dagr dies Iovis*' the day of Jupiter' Thursday *Thursdaeg* 'the day of Thor', from Norse *Thorsdagrdies*

FRIDAY- Veneris 'the day of Venus'. Friday *Frigesdaeg* 'the day of Freya', from Norse *Freyjasdagr*

The Planets

A **Planet** in ancient Rome was referred to as a "Wandering Star", these wandering stars include the north and south Lunar Nodes, (in Latin: Caput Draconis and Caudo Draconis). There are nine planets (five visible) and two luminaries. The extra-

Saturnine planets (Uranus, Neptune and Hades) were not included in the ancient Roman Planets.

The following graph to the Planets is the **Latin and English** name, the **sex** of the planet, the **nature** and the **qualities** of the planets.

Sol or Sun (Male) Angelic-
Soul, king, highly placed persons, vitality, males, father.

Luna or Moon (Female) Angelic-
Emotions, mind, queen, mother, women.

Mavors or Mars (Male) Infernal-
Energetic action, anger, war, conflict and ego.

Mercury (Neutral) Human-
Communication, intellect and anaiysis.

Zeus or Jupiter (Male) Angelic-
Expansion, optimism, great teachers, fortune.

Venus (Female) Human-
Wealth, pleasure and reproduction, beauty.

Saturn (Male) Infernal-
Aging, depression, learning the hard way, career, longevity, delays.

Caput Draconis
North Node (Male) Infernal-
Delusion, darkness and mental anguish.

Caudo Draconis
South Node (Male) Infernal-
Supernatural influences, realm of the dead, detachment.

The 12 Signs

Aries - The first Sign of the Zodiac is Aries, people born under this Sign have forceful personalities, are brave and have good leadership skills. Aries is represented by a ram and is a fire Sign and is ruled by the planet Mars, named for the Roman god of war. Both of these indicate that Arians are unafraid and brave as well as being natural winners. The Overlord of Aries is the Goddess Minerva.

Taurus - The second Sign is Taurus. Represented by a bull, people born under this Sign are stubborn and persistent. Ruled by Venus, the Roman Goddess of love, Taureans like beauty and harmony. As an Earth Sign, Taureans are practical, dependable and conservative. They will finish one project before taking on another. The Overlord of Taurus is the Goddess Maia.

Gemini - The third Sign is an air Sign, ruled by Mercury, named after the Greek messenger God, and represented by twins. Gemini's are intellectual and talkative and generally always see two sides in a situation. They are quick witted and full of energy. This energy makes them appear unfocused. The Overlords of Gemini are the Gods Dioscuri.

Cancer - The fourth Sign is represented by the crab. People born under this Sign are homely, domestic and nurturing, ruled by the Moon. A water Sign, Cancerians can be very emotional and, to the extreme, can be vengeful towards anyone who causes them (or their families) pain or upset. The Overlord of Cancer is the Goddess Artemis.

Leo - Leo is ruled by the lion, king of the jungle. People born under this Sign are born leaders and like to think of themselves as authoritative figures. Being ruled by the Sun, Leo's like to be the center of attention and very often succeed. Leo is a fire Sign which explains why they are always eager to jump into a project and lead the way. They are also loyal and dignified. The Overlord of Leo is the God Aether.

Virgo - The indulgent and fussy sixth Sign is represented by a virgin. Virgos can be modest and practical. An Earth Sign ruled by Mercury, Virgos are down to earth and can be over skeptical but usually very reliable. The Overlord of Virgo is the Goddess Persephone (Core).

Libra - The balanced seventh Sign, ruled by Venus, is represented by scales. With this mix, Librans are bound to enjoy beautiful things. Librans tend to enjoy high arts, intelligent conversation and fairness although they can come across as lazy while they are more interested in making their world beautiful than in practical pursuits. The Overlord of Libra is the God Amor.

Scorpio - The eighth Sign is the scorpion. People born under this Sign are curious and like to be in control, which can cause them to be stubborn and overbearing. Scorpios are ruled by Mars and also by Hades. Being ruled by the God of war, as well as the God of the underworld, makes Scorpios motivated and focused. Being a water Sign, they can be emotional but, unlike other water Signs, Scorpios tend to not show their emotions. The Overlord of Scorpio is the Goddess Hecate.

Sagittarius - The ninth Sign is the birth date of the nomadic Sagittarians. Their symbol is the centaur, known as an intellectual half man, half beast in Roman mythology. Sagittarians are thinkers and love information, especially pertaining to theology and philosophy. Sagittarius is ruled by Jupiter, Roman ruler of the Gods, and people born under this Sign are very lucky and optimistic. Their element is fire which leads them to be sporadic in nature but also inspirational. The Overlord of Sagittarius is the God Apollo.

Capricorn - The tenth Sign is an earth Sign ruled by Saturn - father of many Gods in Roman mythology. These elements make Capricorns hardworking and ambitious. Represented by the goat, Capricorns like to be at the top of any given project as they patiently await their glory, at the same time, realizing they must sometimes rely on other people to reach their goal. The Overlord of Capricorn is the God Pan.

Aquarius - The eleventh Sign, ruled by Saturn and Uranus, Aquarius is an air Sign. Saturn was the father of many Roman Gods and Uranus was the oldest of the Roman Gods. This combination makes people born under this Sign strong, stern and inventive. Added to the intellectual air Sign, Aquarians can accomplish almost anything. Represented by the water carrier, Aquarians may have gifts in technology. The Overlord of Aquarius is the God Oceanus.

Pisces - Represented by a pair of fish, Piscean's often embody a sensible nature. As the twelfth and final Sign, Pisces interestingly intertwines many of the characteristics from the other eleven Signs. People born under this Sign are highly emotional and tend to put great importance on their emotional well-being; they are very spiritual, which commonly is directly associated with their dreams and psychic ability. Pisces is ruled by two planets, Neptune (ruler of the sea) and Jupiter (ruler of the sky). This, along with their element of water, makes them very spiritual and emotional although they can become pessimistic and over sensitive at times. The Overlord of Pisces is the Goddess Venus.

In addition to being ruled by the planets, each zodiac Sign is classified by its nature or essence. There are 4 Cardinal Signs, 4 Fixed Signs, and 4 Mutable Signs in the zodiac.

Cardinal: As with the Cardinal directions, North, South, East, and West, Cardinal Signs in astrology are oriented to the four general seasons: Spring, Summer, Fall, and Winter. Cardinal Signs (Aries, Cancer, Libra, and Capricorn) tend to be people who take action. They take initiative and jump right in; they are motivated and enterprising. However, although they always get a running start, they may fail to complete projects and leave unfinished work in their wakes.

Fixed: People who fall into the Fixed category (Taurus, Leo, Scorpio, and Aquarius) are people who crave stability. They want to own things and be the boss. They want other people to do the activity while they remain still, but they will stubbornly see to it that a project is completed, no matter how long it takes or who they have to push. They can be inflexible, but will hold their stance even under pressure.

Mutable: Mutable Signs (Gemini, Virgo, Sagittarius, and Pisces) are communicators and mediators. They will usually compromise and will listen to both sides of an issue. When they are interested, they will remain with a job or in a relationship indefinitely, but if they become bored, they will leave and not turn back. They are adaptable, but can be inconsistent.

Earth: People with an earth Sign influence (Taurus, Virgo, Capricorn) are well-grounded and down-to-earth. They are hard workers and get the job done; they are not risk takers and prefer a steady, stable path. They are reliable, dutiful, conservative, logical, and responsible. They appreciate all that can be seen and touched, and like to accumulate worldly possessions. They love the finer things in life and will strive to situate themselves accordingly. Under unfavorable aspects, they may become greedy and too materialistic, stepping upon others to gratify themselves.

Air: People with an air Sign influence (Gemini, Libra, Aquarius) are smart and enterprising. They love a puzzle or dilemma and will find unique solutions. They are inventive and think out of the box; they are generally optimistic and tend to think of the glass as half full. They thrive on processing information and are curious and alert. On the down side, they can be cold and calculating, not fully understanding the emotional needs of others.

Fire: People with a fire Sign influence (Aries, Leo, Sagittarius) are self-sufficient, courageous risk takers. People born under this Sign approach life with gusto and tend to be aggressive in their personal relationships. They are considered to be the most desirable of the elements. They are fun, engaging and creative in all aspects of their lives; however, they can also be terribly selfish, demanding and bossy under unfavorable conditions, and often refuse to see other viewpoints but their own when confronted with an issue. They can be very headstrong and like to bully their way through life if it they don't get what they want.

Water: People with a water Sign influence (Cancer, Scorpio, Pisces) are the "feelers" of the world. They are extremely intuitive, compassionate, profoundly receptive and are known to have psychic abilities. They are artistic and love beautiful things. They form strong emotional bonds with others and are always willing to help. They are caring and also enjoy when others care for them in return. On the down side, they can be moody and may tend to dwell on the bad things.

Gods, Angels and Astrology

Gods play an important role in Roman/Greco Astrology because ninety percent of the Gods (angels) exist in the subtle or power realm. When someone is born, the God/Goddess which rules over the Star of that particular day is hard at work and stamps the individual with his/her inner essence.

The Gods are separated into three different categories based upon their individual duties. The three categories are: Angelic, Human or Infernal and when a person is born, he/she will possess the qualities of the God that rules over that day. In Astrology, this is called the "Nature" of the Star.

The first category or nature is called **Angelic**. Angelic personalities are vibrant, loyal and have a preference to keep their minds and bodies clean. Angelic personalities deal with **perseverance**. They are attracted to things of beauty and prefer the finer things in life. The Lord of all the Angelic personalities is Apollo, the Sun God.

Angelic Stars: Dioscuri, Prometheus, Artemis, Zeus, Sol, Favonius, Urania, Hermaia and Apollo

The second category of Stars is called **Human.** Human Stars are non-dual and tend to strive for balance and unity. Human Stars are earthly, passionate and lean toward expression. The human nature deals with **creation.** The God Bacchus rules over the human nature of the Stars.

Human Stars: Hades, Pasiphae, Typhon, Bacchus, Hymneaeus, Ceto, Natura, Chimera and Phorcus

The third personality is the **Infernal** type. Infernal personalities deal with endings and finalizations as well as destruction. They have to learn tolerance and strength. They deal with things on a deeper level than most and can emotionally struggle due to feeling the intensity of everything. The Goddess Hecate rules over this category.

Infernal Stars: Vesta, Hydra, Persephone, Vulcan, Dinus, Parca , Hecate, Muses and Aegeon.

People who have many planets in Infernal Stars tend to be harsh, different than those who have planets in the Angelic Stars. However we have to keep in mind that Angelic personalities are not necessarily good and Infernal are not necessarily bad. In fact they both have their role to play in creation and are equally important. If Infernal forces did not exist, it would be impossible to deal with our karma. In that case, we would never master who we are, very little spiritual growth would result out of everything being so easy and light. We currently live in a time where the full totality of God is difficult to understand. We call something positive if we enjoy it and negative if we do not. Where, in fact, both are used for the elevation of the spirit. We intuitively know the difficulties in our life have made us who we are today. We know this, but still fall into the trap that God is only good. God is all three faces of creator, preserver and destroyer. In ancient Roman religion the three faces of God or Goddess (Deus/Dea) were as such: Bacchus (male, creator), Apollo (male, preserver) and Typhon (male, destroyer) or Minerva (female, creator), Venus (female, preserver) and Hecate (female, destroyer). All three faces are a necessity to realize and understand the true face of the Divine.

(It is important to note that although Hades and Typhon are infernal gods, they display human traits on those born under their Star).

HECATE, the Goddess of Asterian Astrology

Hecate, daughter of Asteria and the Goddess of Moon Mysteries

But, again, the Moon is Hecate, the symbol of her varying phases and of her power dependent on the phases. Wherefore her power appears in three forms, having as symbol of the new Moon the figure in the white robe and golden sandals, and torches lighted: the basket, which she bears when she has mounted high, is the symbol of the cultivation of the crops, which she makes to grow up according to the increase of her light: and again the symbol of the full Moon is the Goddess of the brazen sandals.- Porphyry

Hecate, the Goddess of the night, is the Queen of Asterian Astrology. She rules over all three "natures" herself. She is the powerful triple Goddess of the Moon (angelic), Earth (human), and Tartarus (underworld). Hecate is the original Moon Goddess, her name means "Far-Darter or Hundred Handed", which is a title also given to Apollo the Sun God whose rays are like arrows, and indeed she was often equated with his archer sister Artemis. Hecate is said to have come from Thrace, and certain philosophers named her daughter of the Titans Perses (by some accounts brother to Circe) and Asteria ("Starry", also an epithet of Venus), both deities of light. As the Moon, Hecate (with Phoebus, the Sun) served as witness when Ceres's daughter Persephone was abducted, since the Moon and Sun see all. Hecate Luna is the form of the Goddess that rules over Astrology. Hecate is the Goddess that shows up at the moment of birth and stamps the soul with the karma of that life. The second a new born baby takes his/her first breath, Hecate infuses the spirit with all the impressions of the previous life.

As an earth Goddess, Hecate can grant wealth and riches. As Hecate Trivia "Goddess of Crossroads", she protects crossroads, especially those where three roads meet, and is shown in triple form standing back to back to back, sighting down each road. She also protects travelers, especially those in lonely places and in solitude.

As Goddess of the Underworld, Hecate was said to wait on Queen Persephone, and associated with spirits, ghosts and hounds. She also had great powers of magic. On Earth, she was known to haunt tombs and places where crimes occurred, and was followed by her ghostly train and spectral hounds. Though humans could not see her, earthly dogs always could. Offerings of food were left to her on the last day of the month in the Roman lunar calendar, at the dark of the Moon.

(more on Hecate)

Her three forms (trimorphos) and her three faces (triposopos) make her, as in classical Greek tradition, the Goddess of crossroads (triodites) and the protectress of roads; but they express above all the "abundance of all magical Signs", possessed by the "sovereign" Goddess (kuria) "of many names" (poluonumos). Sometimes the three-faced Hecate are depicted as animals, the love charm of Pitys, has the head of a cow on the right, the head of a female dog on the left, and the head of a girl in the center. The Hecate engraved in a magnetized rock also shows three faces: a goat on the right, a female dog on the left, and in the middle a girl with horns. Her mouth exhales fire (puripnoa); her six hands brandish torches. The fire that inhabits Hecate, as the most subtle of the four elements, characterizes her keen intelligence and the extreme sharpness of her perception (puriboulos). Her whole being radiates with the brilliance of the fire from the stars and from the ether. The Chaldaean Oracles made this Hecate "of the breasts that welcome storms, of resplendent brilliance" into an entity "descended from the Father," associated with the "implacable thunderbolts" of the Gods, with the "flower of fire," and with the "powerful breath" of the paternal Intellect. Because she caries and transmits fire from above, she is the supreme Goddess of vivification. The reason Hecate's womb is so remarkably "fertile" (zoogonon) is that she is filled with the fire of paternal Intellect, the source of life or the strength of thought, which it is her duty to communicate and to disseminate. Through her emblems and her triadic conception, Hecate is associated with another Goddess of time and destiny, Mene or Selene, the

Goddess of the Moon. A prayer to the Moon invokes them as one and the same entity; epithets and attributes of the two Goddesses are interchangeable. Hecate/Selene also has three heads, carries torches, presides over crossroads: "You who in the three forms of the three Charites dance and fly about with the stars . . . You who wield awful black torches in your hands, you who shake your head with hair made of fearsome snakes, you who cause the bellowing of the bulls, you whose belly is covered with reptilian scales and who carry over your shoulder a woven bag of venomous snakes". She has the eyes of a bull, the voice of a pack of dogs, the calves of a lion, the ankles of a wolf, and she loves fierce dogs: "This is why you are called Hecate of many names, Mene you who split the air like Artemis, shooter of arrows". She is the mother (geneteria) of Gods and men, Nature the universal mother (Phusis panmetor): "You come and go on Olympus and visit the vast and immense Abys: you are the beginning and end, you alone rule over all things; it is in you that all originates, and in you, eternal, that all ends". Another hymn in the Paris codex used as a love charm shows the same joy in piling up titles of the Goddess, who has this time become Venus, the universal procreator (pangenneteria) and mother of Eros, at once below and above, "in the Hells, the Abyss, and the Aeon", chthonic, holding her feasts in tombs, and associated with Ereskigal, the Babylonian queen of Hells, but also the "celestial traveler among the stars". Her ring, scepter and crown represent the power of the one who, possessing the triad, embraces all. Above and below, to the right and to the left, at night as during the day, she is the one "Around whom the nature of the world turns", the very Soul of the world, according to the Chaldaean Oracle "the center in the middle of the Fathers", occupying, according to Psellos, an intermediary position and playing the role of the center in relation to all the *other powers: to her left the source of virtues, to her right the source of souls, inside, because she remains within her own substance, but also directed to the outside with a view to procreation.*

To the Christian Gnostics, who believed that magic had been brought to earth by angels and spirits, Hecate represents one of the five Archons appointed to rule over the 360 deities of the "Middle," the aerial place below the zodiacal sphere or the circle of the Sun, which fixes the Heimarmene. She has three faces and 27 deities under her command. She occupies the third level in the hierarchy of the "Middle," between two female deities, long-haired Paraplex and Ariouth the Ethiopian, and two male Gods, Typhon and Iachtanabas (Pisitis Sophia).- Roman Book of Laws

This last paragraph reveals that Hecate was seen as the Goddess of Greco Astrology. In ancient India and Greece, there were 360 days in the year and ancient culture believed a different deity ruled over each day of the year (this is still followed in India to this day). One of the many reasons for Hecate having three faces was based upon her connection to the three major phases of the Moon and the three phases inside the 27 lunar mansions (Stars). The Moon transits from a South Node Star to a Mercury Star three times to complete her journey through the Lunar Zodiac. The 27 deities under her command are the 27 Stars which are addressed in this book. Hecate was the Queen of the Night and the Moon, therefore Hecate, the great mystery "Trivia", cannot be anything other than the Goddess of the hidden system of Asterian Astrology.

Hecate was also named the Heimarmene (Destiny) in ancient Rome and Greece which was the force responsible for imprinting you with your fate and your celestial personality.

The 27 STARS

These interpretations are taken directly from the Yavanajataka 2,300 years ago.

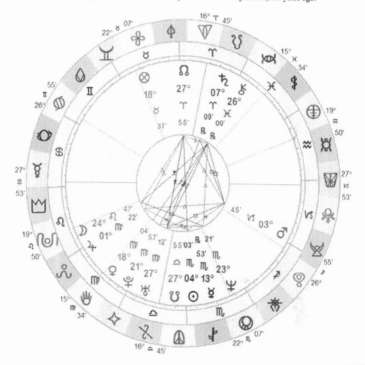

All solar dates listed under them Stars are for 2010, if you are born on a cusp, please locate a sidereal ephemeris to find your Star.

1. DIOSCURI (HORSE) April 13th to April 26th

Sign: 0' Aries to 13'20 Aries

Lord: South Node

God: Dioscuri

Nature: Angelic

Animal: Horse

Body Part: top of feet

GOD:

The Dioscuri were star-crowned twin Gods; their appearances on the rigging of a ship were believed to assist in the escape from storms. The Dioscuri were depicted as beardless youths, horsemen wearing wide-brimmed traveler's hats. They were also Gods of horsemanship, healers and protectors of guests and travelers.

The twins were born as mortal princes, sons of the Spartan Queen Leda, one born from King Tyndareus (the Queen Leda's husband) and the other by Zeus. As the twins evolved, they showed generosity and kindness to man so they were asked to take on the difficult job of being the Gods of death. Polydeukes (the first born twin), son of Zeus, was initially offered this gift, but he agreed only on condition that his half-twin Castor share the honor. Zeus assented, but the pair had to spend alternate days in Hades to appease the Fates and the Gods of the Dead.

The Dioscuri received a placement among the stars as the Constellation Gemini (the Twins). Their alternations between Heaven and Hades may refer to the heavenly cycles - their constellation is visible in the heavens for only six months of the year.

STAR:

The Dioscuri are rare because they rule over the Constellation Gemini as well as this Lunar Mansion. The Dioscuri rule over death and have a healing side; they are known to be the physician of the Gods. The symbol of Dioscuri is the head of a horse.

This Lunar Mansion assigns zeal, energy, magnetic personality and courage. Those who are born in this Lunar Mansion are generally attractive and elegant. Dioscuri borne, move, think and act very fast. At times their love for speeding can cause them trouble instead of efficiency. They initiate new things and projects constantly. Here, the qualities of a horse are displayed wherever this Star makes its mark. Dioscuri people enjoy positive interaction in personal relationships, except their stubbornness can create turmoil. The heroic and courageous nature of all the people born under this star comes in handy while choosing professions like armed forces, law enforcement etc. Love for speeding also lends an interest in sports, athletics, flying, riding and business (quick thinking). This Star also provides the natives with healing capabilities, and one can progress to great heights in medicine and alternate fields thereof. They are scrupulous, prosperous, obedient, truthful, and obtain all comforts. They are endowed with good family and children and wealth. They are daring, attractive and well off. They are capable administrators, and are often respected. They sacrifice money, have a good conduct and greatly enjoy life.

They are quick and candid, a knower of philosophy, rational and succeed in quarrels. They have nice hands and wide eyes. They are respected by Kings and speak sweetly. If Dioscuri is afflicted with Saturn or Mars, they can become daring, arrogant, thievish, and fraudulent. An affliction to this Star can make them unkind and can make them gravitate towards lower actions.

This symbol mimics the traditional Sign for Dioscuri, a horse's head. This Star represents the head, or the beginning of the zodiac. This symbol also resembles the female reproductive system. Dioscuri relates to all initiations and beginnings.

Moon/Sun in:

Dioscuri indicates a person who is a pioneer, innovator and explorer, who is heroic, courageous, restless, impatient, with a zest for life. They have a strong desire to be of service to others. They are energetic and magnetic, quick in speech and actions. However, they can also be inconsiderate and irresponsible.

2. HADES (ELEPHANT) April 27th to May 10th

Sign: 13' 20 Aries to 26'40 Aries

Lord: Venus

God: Hades

Nature: Human

Animal: Elephant

Body Part: Bottom of Feet

GOD:

Hades (or Pluto) was the King of the Underworld, the God of death and all deceased. He presided over funeral rites and defended the right of the dead. Hades was also the God of hidden treasures in the earth. Hades was devoured by Saturnus as soon as he was born, along with four of his siblings. Zeus later caused the Titan to disgorge them, and together they drove the Titan Gods from heaven and locked them away in the pit of Tartaros. Then the three victorious brothers drew lots for the division of the cosmos; Hades received the third portion, the dark dismal realm of the underworld, as his domain.

Hades desired a bride and petitioned his brother Zeus to grant him one of his daughters. Zeus offered him Persephone, the daughter of Ceres. However, knowing Persephone would resist the marriage, Zeus consented to a forceful abduction of her. When Ceres learned of this, she was furious and caused a great chaos to fall upon the earth until her daughter was returned. Zeus was compelled to concede or else mankind would perish so the girl was fetched forth from the Underworld. However, Persephone mistakenly ate from a pomegranate seed and consequently was forced to return to Hades for a portion of each year.

Hades was depicted as a dark-bearded, regal God. He was depicted as either Hades, enthroned in the Underworld, holding a bird-tipped scepter, or as Plouton, the giver of wealth, pouring fertility from a cornucopia. The Romans also named him Dis.

STAR:

This star is under the planetary Lordship of Venus and is within the Sign of Aries, ruled by Mars. Hades represents the character of the Underworld. Hades's animal symbol is the elephant. This star is connected with the energies we expend to maintain ourselves in the material world. This Star endows creative and mental inclinations to the person born in it. The person is intelligent, witty and constantly dealing with ideologies of his own or others. A fanatic loyalty to ones own thinking, usually creating courageous people who fight for their beliefs. The same tendency can lead to cases where this Star borne feels restricted by other's opinions, and thus can become a bitter opponent. This Star causes one to go through ups and downs in life and will constantly create opportunities to renovate life. Whether a person uses the opportunity or not is entirely in his/her hand. In spite of having Hades as their deity, people of this Star generally live quite long. Endowed by medium build and fine teeth, the subjects do have love for fine things in life. They are connoisseurs and even artistically inclined as painters, and musicians. Careers in military, chemicals and medicine are lucrative for the people borne under this Star, as it sits in the Sign of Aries.

The full Moon in Hades indicates Halloween. The veil of the dead opens and this full Moon grants the ability to interact with deceased loved ones. This full Moon can also indicate a great change in the particular House the Moon falls under (in the Natal chart), and this change will persist throughout the month.

People born in this Star are likely to incur the displeasure of others. They have scars on their body due to injuries and suffer from various diseases. They are known to fear bodies of water. They are enjoyers, obedient and learned; they know religion, rationale, intelligent and win in quarrels. They are good speakers, stable, knowledgeable and truthful. They are long lived. They are also determined, and proud, they do not tolerate human ignorance.

Hades is the Star of birth, death and transformation. The symbol is a vagina. The triangle references three stars which compose this Star. These three stars, also known as "the Buckle of Isis", were perceived by ancient astrologers as portals between worlds.

Moon/Sun in:

Hades indicates a person who suffers, struggles, is restrained and experiences obstacles in life. They often can be resentful of these restrictions. They are known to inflict their beliefs on others, or else fight to liberate themselves and others from oppression. They are intelligent and witty and love the finer things in life, but they can also be fanatical in their beliefs, which can lead to severe ups and downs in life.

3. VESTA (RAM) May 11th to May 23rd

Sign: 26'40 Aries to 10' Taurus

Lord: Sun

God: Vesta

Nature: Infernal

Body Part: Head

Animal: Ram

GOD:

Vesta was the virgin Goddess of the hearth (both private and municipal) and the home. As the Goddess of the family hearth she also presided over the cooking of bread and the preparation of the family meal. Vesta was also the Goddess of the sacrificial flame and she received a share of every sacrifice to the Gods. The cooking of the communal feast of sacrificial meat was naturally a part of her domain. (sacrifice: meaning that they gave thanks to the animal before eating it.)

In the myth of Vesta, she was the first born child of Saturnus (her father) and Ops (her mother), and she was swallowed by her father at birth. Zeus later forced the old Titan to disgorge Vesta and her siblings. As the first to be swallowed she was also the last to be disgorged, and so was named as both the eldest and youngest of the six Cronides. When the Gods Sol and Neptune sought for her hand in marriage, Vesta refused and asked Zeus to let her remain an eternal virgin. He agreed and she took her place at his royal hearth.

Vesta was depicted in a Minervian vase painting as a modestly veiled woman sometimes holding a flowered branch. In classical sculpture she was also veiled, with a kettle as her attribute.

STAR:

Vesta is also known as the "star of fire" and is related to a commander, fighter, foster mother, luster, power, physical and creative force. Vesta being a female Star suggests passivity, indicating that Vesta needs outer energy or life circumstance to activate their power. People borne in this constellation are also very fiery in nature. They have a very strong personality, which at times can intimidate other people. At other times, the fire is well placed under placid exterior. Vesta borne native is generally an aggressive, focused, driven individual with a sharp mind and cutting tongue. There is a protective streak about people born under this Lunar Mansion. Whether it is about shielding their loved ones, adopting and nurturing an orphan, or fighting for the underdog, Vesta people surely shine. People born under this influence have magnetic personality and stand out in the crowd. They are also good at excelling through persistence. Therefore they can be placed in multiple professions; yet careers in engineering, law, military, business and interior decoration, marketing and human resources are often favorable.

Vesta is traditionally denoted by a blade or a flame. This symbol combines the two motifs, expressing this Star's sharp, proactive nature.

Moon/Sun in:

Vesta borne are outgoing and love friends and family; endowed with children, enjoy life and are very prosperous. They can struggle with money at times because they also enjoy spending frivolously. They love travel but deny the help rendered by others. They can be harsh, and get caught in doing emotionally or physically difficult jobs. They are bright, easy to anger and passionate. They are heavy eaters and can be fiery. They are stingy, intelligent, famous, successful, and loved by their partner.

4. PASIPHAE (SNAKE) May 24th to June 09th

Sign: 10' Taurus to 23'20 Taurus

Lord: Moon

God: Luna

Nature: Human

Animal: Snake

Body Part: Forehead

GOD:

Luna was the Titan Goddess of the Moon. She was depicted as a woman either riding side saddle on a horse or in a chariot drawn by a pair of winged steeds. Her lunar sphere or crescent was represented as either a crown set upon her head or as the fold of a raised, shining cloak. Sometimes she was said to drive a team of oxen and her lunar crescent was likened to the horns of a bull. Luna's great love was the shepherd prince Endymion. The beautiful boy was granted eternal youth and immortality by Zeus and placed in a state of eternal slumber in a cave near the peak of Lydian Mount Latmos. There his heavenly bride Luna descended to consort with him in the night.

A number of other Goddesses were also associated with the Moon; however, only Luna was represented by the old Greek poets as the Moon incarnate. Other Greek Moon Goddesses included Pasiphae, Leukippides, Eileithyia, Hecate, Artemis,

Bendis, and Juno (whom sometimes doubled for Luna in the Endymion myth).

STAR:

Those born in Pasiphae are agriculturists, experts, well-behaved, attractive, good speakers and poets. Pasiphae evokes some degree of jealousy because others may resent their gains. This Star indicates strong desire which should be expressed in creative ways. Out of the 27 Stars, the Moon enjoys this Star the most, due to Luna being the queen of the Moon. She is said to be gorgeous, seductive, pampered, and fond of fine and beautiful things in life. Much similar to her characteristics, people born in Pasiphae are elegant, passionate and most likely have a good sex drive. They often won't hesitate to use their charisma to gain whatever they want in life. Pasiphae people possess a love for the arts, music, fine clothes and luxury. They attract respect and admiration quite naturally; at times, this is the reason they become insensitive and critical towards the unfortunate. Otherwise, natives are usually very well behaved people. The professions suited to people born under this Star are: politics, writing, acting, arts, and agriculture. They are of sweet-speech, intelligent, capable and bright. They are long-lived, involved in socially accepted jobs, religious, truthful and help those who have helped them. People of power respect them. They are endowed with good looking limbs and a wide forehead, handsome, independent, usually respected by the higher class, loved by their children, interested in wealth and enjoy money.

Pasiphae is represented by a four-pedaled flower. This relates to its connection to the number four, as well as its typical emblem, the rose. Pasiphae relates to Taurine themes of stability and abundance.

Moon/Sun in:

Pasiphae indicates a person who is passionate, sexually seductive, elegant, attractive and charismatic. They love children, art, music and luxury, and the fine things of life, but can be snobbish, pampered, materialistic and critical of those whom they consider not up to their own standards.

5. PROMETHEUS (SNAKE) June 10th to June 20th

Sign: 26'20 Taurus to 6'40 Gemini

Lord: Mars

God: Prometheus

Nature: Angelic

Animal: Snake

Body Part: Eyebrows

GOD:

Prometheus was the Titan God of forethought and crafty counsel; he was entrusted with the task of molding mankind out of clay. His attempts to better the lives of his creation brought him into direct conflict with Zeus. First he tricked the Gods out of the best portion of the sacrificial feast, acquiring the meat for the feasting of man. Then, when Zeus withheld fire, he stole it from heaven and delivered it to mortal kind hidden inside a fennel-stalk. As punishment for these rebellious acts, Zeus ordered the creation of Pandora (the first woman) as a means to deliver misfortune into the House of man, or as a way to cheat mankind out of the company of the good spirits. Prometheus meanwhile, was arrested and bound to a stake on Mount Kaukasos where an eagle was set to feed upon his ever-regenerating liver (or, some say, heart). Generations later the great hero Heracles came along and released the old Titan from his torture.

STAR:

Prometheus borne like to roam about in forests and nature, they love life and seek knowledge or excitement. Prometheus is partly in Taurus and partly in Gemini. It conveys the ideas of searching for beauty. People born in this Star have a strong body and moderate complexion. This Star depicts curiosity or searching. A search for something newer and more brilliant keeps the people born in the Star revved up for new experiences and opportunities in life. Prometheus people are gentle like a deer, with equally attractive appearance. But internally they are constantly searching for something. People of this Star are either researchers, scientists or in other professions tempted by changes and adventures. They are good public speakers, intelligent, and friendly. People born in this Star have a natural attraction for opposite sex, and are constantly pushing their limits to have romantic affairs. This Star also speaks of motherly instincts. They are devoted to their mothers. Career avenues imbibing constant changes are ideal for Prometheus borne. They are great at sports, the travel industry, and are attracted to professions in the media.

This symbol emulates Prometheus's cup of elixir. It also combines the symbols for Taurus and Gemini, the two zodiac Signs which correspond to this Star. The curved line which reflects the horns of Taurus may also be interpreted as symbolic of Prometheus's other motif, the deer.

Moon/Sun in:

Prometheus indicates a person who is restless and nervous, constantly searching or looking for something. They are gentle, tender, peaceful, sensual and romantic, with motherly instincts. They are always curious and make great travelers, investigators, researchers and collectors, as well as good public speakers and communicators. This Star also deals with gems, sculpting and making beautiful things with their hands.

6. TYPHON (DOG) June 21st to July 4th

Sign: 6'40 Gemini to 20' Gemini

Lord: North Node

God: Typhon

Nature: Human

Animal: Dog

Body Part: Eyes

GOD:

Typhon (or Typhoeus) was a monstrous immortal storm-giant who was defeated and imprisoned by Zeus in the pit of Tartarus. He was the source of devastating storm winds which issued forth from that dark nether realm.

Later poets described him as a volcanic-demon, trapped beneath the body of Mount Aitna in Sicily. In this guise he was closely identified with the Gigante Enkelados.

Typhon was so huge that his head was said to brush the stars. He appeared man-shaped down to the thighs, with two coiled vipers in place of his legs. Attached to his hands in place of fingers were a hundred serpent heads, fifty per hand. He was winged, with dirty matted hair and beard, pointed ears, and eyes flashing fire. According to some he had two hundred hands each with fifty serpents for fingers and a hundred heads, one in human form with the rest being heads of bulls, boars, serpents, lions and leopards. As a volcano-demon, Typhon hurled red-hot rocks at the sky and storms of fire boiled from his mouth.

STAR:

When the Sun enters Typhon the earth begins its menstrual course. This Star signifies destruction and sorrow, just like its deity Typhon. Typhon is the destructive part of God. Destruction is necessary for regeneration, and fertility. Hence, the intention of this Star is always creativity. Typhon born people are usually stubborn, who, with kindness, easily dominate others. But these people can also be gentle, sympathetic, and can command the situations around them effectively. They have stable and strong personalities and are extremely effective in getting things done. They like to renovate discarded things. People born in this Star can suitably direct their energies to difficult and transformative professions.

The symbol of Typhon combines two emblems; the diamond and the raindrop (or teardrop). Together, they provide a visual description of Typhon's theme of growth and renewal through chaos and turbulence.

Moon/Sun in:

Typhon indicates a person who is skilled at creating new things out of the old. They are usually leaders; however they can be cold, calculating, stubborn and controlling with shifting temperaments. On the other hand, they can also be strong, stable and have sympathetic personalities. This Star creates great communicators and talented writers.

7. ARTEMIS (CAT) July 5th to July 18th

Sign: 20' Gemini to 3'30 Cancer

Lord: Jupiter

God: Artemis

Nature: Angelic

Animal: Cat

Body Part: Nose

GOD:

Artemis was the great Olympian Goddess of hunting, wilderness and wild animals. She was also a Goddess of childbirth, and a protector of women from childhood up to marriage. Her twin brother Sol was similarly the protector of male children.

In ancient art Artemis was usually depicted as a girl dressed in a short knee-length chiton equipped with a hunting bow and quiver of arrows.

Artemis of the Greeks was identified with Roman Diana; both share a peculiar tripartite characteristic which strongly marks the individuality of the Greek Goddess. In heaven she was Luna (the Moon), on earth Artemis (the huntress-Goddess), and in the lower world Persephone. Unlike the Ephesian Artemis, Artemis in her character as Persephone, carries no element of love or sympathy into the lower world, she is, on the contrary, characterized by practices altogether hostile to man.

STAR:

Artemis brings about the return of energy and vitality. It causes our creative growths and inspirations to be renewed. After the bleak and destructive storms of Typhon, the element of light returned. This is a very pious Star, which gives intellect and honor to the person born in it. It also gives courage to pursue ones ideals and ambition. This Star lends an inclination towards spirituality and faith. Artemis people are honest and truthful to the core. One of the beauties of this Star is that even if a person loses everything in life; he/she can rise again like a phoenix, and rebuild his/her life. They have limitless inner resources, and no limitations to what they can achieve. This is a very prosperous Star, in spite of the fact that the native is not so materialistically inclined. The Artemis borne truly value family; consequently, their families are very fortunate to have them around. The people of this Star lean towards humanitarian careers. Diet and health are priorities. They can also be brilliant writers, journalists, and actors.

Artemis's symbol relates to themes of retrieving, recovering, and recycling. This Star is traditionally denoted by a quiver of arrows (magical weapons which return after fulfilling their mission). These arrows are depicted here in their circular path from beginning to return.

Moon/Sun in:

Artemis indicates a person with strong inner resources and ability to bounce back from difficulties, is philosophical, religious, spiritual, likeable, charming and forgiving. They are idealistic, truthful to the core and value home life.

8. ZEUS (RAM) July 19th to August 1st

Sign: 3'20 Cancer to 16'40 Cancer

Lord: Saturn

God: Zeus

Nature: Angelic

Animal: Ram

Body Part: Face

GOD:

Zeus was the king of the Gods, the God of sky and weather, law, order and fate. He was depicted as a regal man, mature with a sturdy figure and dark beard. His usual attributes were a lightning bolt, royal scepter and eagle.

Zeus, the great presiding deity of the universe, the ruler of heaven and earth, was regarded by the Romans, first, as the God of all rules, secondly, as the personification of the laws of nature, thirdly, as Lord of state-life, and fourthly, as the father of Gods and men.

As the God of weather phenomena he could produce storms, tempests, and intense darkness. At his command the mighty thunder rolls, the lightning flashes, and the clouds open and pour forth their refreshing streams to fructify the earth.

As the personification of the operations of nature, he represents those grand laws of unchanging and harmonious order, by which not only the physical but also the moral world is governed. Hence he is the God of regulated time as marked by the changing seasons, and by the regular succession of day and night, in contradistinction to his father Cronus, who represents all time.

STAR:

Zeus borne like to nourish, preserve, protect, replenish, multiply and strengthen. This is considered to be one of the best Stars of all. The natives born in this Star are intelligent, spiritual and selfless. They attract wealth (often up to the point of opulence) as their karmic reward. Zeus borne people are self sufficient, deep thinkers and philosophers. They care deeply about others and try to uplift the conditions of people around them. They work for the underprivileged, and spread their knowledge through teaching. Sometimes the same streak can take the form of arrogance, as one tends to think him superior from others. Still, to be born under this Star is truly priceless. People of this constellation do well in fields of social service, medicine, and teaching.

Zeus is the Star of nourishment, generosity and kindness. Its symbol is a circle which can be seen as a wheel, a drop of milk, a coconut, or the Moon inside a blossoming lotus flower.

Moon/Sun in:

Zeus indicates a person who is religious, conventional, helpful, selfless, caring, intelligent and spiritual. They are usually self-sufficient and wealthy, but enjoy community service. However, they can be arrogant and superior towards those who do not share their high ideals.

9. HYDRA (CAT) August 2nd to August 15th

Sign: 16'40 Cancer to 30' Cancer

Lord: Mercury

God: Hydra

Nature: Infernal

Animal: Cat

Body Part: Ears

GOD:

Hydra was a gigantic, seven-headed water-serpent, which haunted the swamps of Lerna. Herakles was sent to destroy her as one of his twelve labors, but for each of her heads which he decapitated, two more sprang forth. So with the help of Iolaos, he applied burning brands to the severed stumps, cauterizing the wounds and preventing regeneration. In the battle he also crushed a giant crab beneath his heel which had come to assist Hydra. Afterwards, the Hydra and the Crab were placed amongst the stars by Juno as the Constellations Hydra and Cancer.

STAR:

The force of Hydra can be understood specifically by its name. Hydra can be helpful if others have enemies, however it can also give a person an inimical temperament as well. It all depends upon how the energy of this Star is used. Hydra is the creature with poisonous capabilities, intensity and a secret nature. Snakes also depict wisdom and a supreme form of spiritual power. Hydra people are very intense, secretive, and sexual; they often get exactly what they want. They can be extremely competitive and openly fierce in their arguments, and can often exploit spiritual power for recognition. If given to their negative tendencies, they can be very bad avengers and manipulators. Their inherent wisdom makes them quite adept in astrology, communications and psychology.

Hydra is two serpentine lines symmetrically entwining, recalling Mercury's healing staff as well as the double-helix pattern of DNA molecule. This powerful Star gives intuition and transformative potential.

Moon/Sun in:

Hydra indicates a person is penetrating, intense, hypnotic and wise. Straightforward, smart, of grand vision, independent, ambitious, bright speaker, commanding respect, skilled in politics, powerful communicator, diplomatic, loves travel. This Star can also be perverse and can carry grudges endlessly. They are known to always attack their opponents as they suffer continual negative memories of their past.

10. PERSEPHONE (RAT) August 16th to August 29th

Sign: 0' Leo to 13'20 Leo

Lord: South Node

God: Persephone

Nature: Infernal

Animal: Rat

Body Part: Lips and Chin

GOD:

Persephone was the Queen of the Underworld, wife of the God Hades. She was also the Goddess of spring growth, who was worshipped alongside her mother Ceres in the Eleusinian Mysteries. This agricultural-based cult promised its initiates passage to a blessed afterlife.

Persephone was titled Core (the Maiden) as the Goddess of spring's bounty. Once upon a time when she was playing in a flowery meadow with her Nymph companions, Core was seized by Hades and carried off to the underworld as his bride. Her mother Ceres despaired at her disappearance and searched for her throughout the world accompanied by the Goddess Hecate bearing torches. When Ceres learned that Zeus had conspired in her daughter's abduction she was furious and refused to let the earth prosper until Persephone was returned. Zeus consented, but because the girl had tasted the food of Hades (a handful of pomegranate seeds) she was forced to spend a part of each year for eternity with her husband in the underworld. Her annual return to the earth in spring was marked by the flowering of the meadows and the sudden growth of the new grain. Her return to the underworld in winter, conversely, saw the dying down of plants and the halting of growth.

In other myths, Persephone appears exclusively as the queen of the underworld, receiving the likes of Herakles and Orpheus at her court.

Persephone was usually depicted as a young Goddess holding sheaf's of grain and a flaming torch. Sometimes she was shown in the company of her mother Ceres, and the hero Triptolemos, the teacher of agriculture. At other times she appears enthroned beside Hades.

STAR:

Persephone is the cause of brightness, light and rules over the world of the dead, but from a positive ancestral place called the Elysian Fields (whereas Hades and Hecate deal with the dark side of the dead-Tartarus). This Star stands for higher impulses and incentives, the gift of Persephone must always be a noble one. It shows that we are coming to the end of a cycle. Persephone is where great kings and leaders are born. Persephone people have natural leadership skills, along with a great deal of pride related to family roots and ancestry. The restlessness in these people manifests itself in a high urge for success and power. This very drive can also be sprouted from a feeling of insecurity hidden within. The people born in this Star can be arrogant, and selfish. But more usually than not, they are wonderful, amiable, and wise human beings. They are naturally endowed with a balanced, positive outlook and thus, become obvious contenders for high positions in life. Natives of this Star are good at public services, politics, and family businesses.

Persephone coincides with the beginning of Leo and epitomizes the Lion attributes: honor, pride, magnificence, duty, glory, and respect. It is symbolized here by a simple three-pointed crown.

Moon/Sun in:

Persephone indicates a person who is noble, eminent, ambitious and generous, with leadership qualities, strong and traditional values and a drive for power and wealth. They are amiable and have a positive outlook on life. They are loyal and proud of their family and ancestors, but can also be elitist and arrogant.

11. BACCHUS (MINK) August 30th to September 12th

Sign: 13'20 Leo to 26'40 Leo

Lord: Venus

God: Bacchus

Nature: Human

Animal: Mink

Body Part: Right Hand

GOD:

Bacchus was the great Olympian God of wine, vegetation, pleasure and festivity. He was depicted as either an older bearded God or a pretty effeminate, long-haired youth. His symbols included the *thyrsos* (a pine-cone tipped staff), drinking cup, leopard, mink and fruiting vine. He was usually accompanied by a troop of Satyrs and Mainades (female devotees or nymphs).

Bacchus was the youthful, beautiful, but riotous God of wine. He is called both by Greeks and Romans: Bacchus (Bakchos), that is, the noisy God, which was originally a mere epithet or surname of Bacchus, but does not occur till after the time of Herodotus.

The common story, which makes Bacchus a son of Semele by Zeus, runs as follows: Juno, jealous of Semele, visited her in the disguise of a friend or an old woman, and persuaded her to request Zeus to appear to her in the same glory and majesty in which he was accustomed to approach his own wife, Juno. When all entreaties to desist from this request were fruitless, Zeus at length complied, and appeared to her in thunder and lightning. Semele was terrified and overpowered by the sight, and being seized by the fire, she gave premature birth to a child. Zeus saved the child from the flames. Various epithets which are given to the God refer to that occurrence, such as purigenês, mêrorraphês, mêrotraphês and *ianigena*.

STAR:

Bacchus is the symbol of creation. Bacchus brings union and procreation on all levels. This Star's symbol is a bed or hammock, a time of rest and relaxation. This Star speaks of marriage. People of this Star rely much on their inherent luck. They are very relaxed and happy-go-lucky in their life. Bacchus people are blessed with pleasant marital life and children. They enjoy family life as much as they enjoy social life. Natives of this Star are very fond of parties, picnics and social events. Bacchus people are endowed with robust health and passionate nature. They are also inclined towards fine arts. This Star produces many brilliant artists.

Bacchus is the Mansion of comfort, pleasure, delight, and indulgence. It follows Persephone, signifying a period of relaxation following worldly accomplishment. Again, its symbol can be seen as one reclining in a luxurious bed.

Moon/Sun in:

Bacchus indicates someone who is carefree, attractive, sensual, affectionate, sociable, kind, generous and loyal. They are good communicators and influencers of others. They are artistic and relaxed in their approach, but can also be lazy and vain. They have a need to be in relationships and family life is important to them.

12. HYMENAEUS (BULL) September 13thto September 25th

Sign: 26'40 Leo to 10' Virgo

Lord: Sun

God: Hymenaeus

Nature: Human

Animal: Bull

Body Part: Left Hand

GOD:

Hymenaeus was the God of weddings, or more specifically of the wedding hymn which was Sung by the train of the bride as she was led to the House of the groom. Hymenaeus was one among the Erotes, the youthful Gods of love. As one of the Gods of song, he was usually described as a son of Sol and a Muse.

Hymenaeus appears in Roman art as a winged child carrying a bridal torch in his hand, depicting the wedding procession of Herakles and Hebe.

The Attic legends described him as a youth of such delicate beauty, that he could possibly be taken for a girl. He fell in love with a maiden, who refused to listen to him; but in the disguise of a girl he followed her to Eleusis to the festival of Ceres. He, together with the other girls, was carried off by robbers into a distant and desolate country. On their landing, the robbers laid down to sleep, and were killed by Hymenaeus, who now returned to Athens, requesting the citizens to give him his beloved in marriage, if he restored to them the maidens who had been carried off by the robbers. His request was granted, and his marriage was extremely happy. For this reason he was invoked in the hymeneal songs. Another myth is that while he was young, he was killed by the breaking down of his House on his wedding day whence he was afterwards invoked in bridal songs, in order to be propitiated. Some said that at the wedding of Bacchus and Ariadne he sang the bridal hymn, but lost his voice. He is represented in works of art as a youth, but taller and with a more serious expression than Eros, and carrying in his hand a bridal torch.

STAR:

Bacchus and Hymenaeus are known as marriage mansions. Natives of both the Star are best settled in marriage. This is the 12th Star of the zodiac. The Sign Lords are Sun and Mercury, the symbol is a bed. Hymenaeus indicates both the need for union and for organizing the resources gained through it. But this particular Star makes the person more dependent in relationship, which often creates commitment to the wrong relationship as well. The people born in this Star also tend to be fixed and stable, and focus mindedly on their way to success. They are also very friendly and encouraging towards people. Their positive approach to people is an added asset to their successful living. The natives are also known to amass prosperity through marriage.

Hymneaeus Star also represents comfort but with an emphasis on wisdom rather then sensuality. It falls into the latter part of Leo, its symbol relates to that Sign. The circle representing the individual, formerly seen enveloped in the blanket of luxury, here rises up like the Sun.

Moon/Sun in:

Hymenaeus indicates a person who is helpful, kind, friendly, caring, sincere and courageous. They are stable, consistent and focused in their approach to life. They need relationships, family unity, and love humanity in general. However, they can also be dependent in relationships and stubborn.

13. SOL (BUFFALO) September 26th to October 12th

Sign: 10'Virgo to 26'40 Virgo

Lord: Moon

God: Sol

Nature: Angelic

Animal: Buffalo

Body Part: Fingers

GOD:

Sol was the Titan God of the Sun. He was also the guardian of oaths and the God of sight. Sol dwelt in a golden Star located in the River Oceanos at the eastern end of the earth. From there he emerged each dawn driving a chariot drawn by four, fiery winged steeds and crowned with the aureole of the Sun. When he reached the land of the Hesperides (Evenings) in the West, he descended into a golden cup which carried him around the northern streams of Oceanos back to his rising place in the East. Once his son Phaethon attempted to drive the chariot of the Sun, but when he lost control he set the earth on fire. Zeus then struck him down with a thunderbolt.

Sol was depicted as a handsome and usually beardless man, clothed in purple robes and crowned with the shining aureole of the Sun. His Sun-chariot was drawn by four steeds, sometimes winged. Sol was identified with several Gods including fiery Vulcan and light-bringing Apollo.

STAR:

This is the 13th Star of the zodiac. The symbol is a closed hand or fist. Sol gives the ability to achieve our goals in a complete and immediate manner. Sol people are skilled in everything related to hand. They are gifted craftsmen, healers, artists, palmists or careers that involve wit. Sol people are usually endowed with comic and clever wit. They are good entertainers and charmers. The people born in this Star usually suffer a lot of hardships in life early on in their youth. They usually turn their path to spirituality. Sol people are very intelligent, and make genuine and good counselors. Sol people have difficulty forgiving others; they hold onto their routines and their dogmas. However, once they come in touch with their true self, their enlightenment is inevitable.

Sol is symbolized by a human hand. This Star relates to all work and activities done with the hands, including all forms of craftsmanship. One traditional symbol for Sol is the potter's wheel, shown here by an empty circle.

Moon/Sun in:

Sol indicates a person who is skillful with their hands, good at craftsmanship and the arts, healers and massagers. They are clever, witty, entertaining and humorous, and are good speakers and communicators. Their early life may be subject to hardship and restraints; they like routine and security. They are also known to be possessive.

14. VULCAN (TIGER) October 13th to October 22nd

Sign: 26'40 Virgo to 6'40 Libra

Lord: Mars

God: Vulcan

Nature: Infernal

Animal: Tiger

Body Part: Neck

GOD:

Vulcan was the great Olympian God of fire, metalworking, stonemasonry, ornaments and the art of sculpture. He was usually depicted as a bearded man holding a hammer and tongs (the tools of a smith) and riding a donkey.

Vulcan is the God of fire, mostly because he manifests himself as a power of physical nature in volcanic districts; he is the indispensable means in arts and manufactures. In Rome, fire was known as the breath of Vulcan, and his name was synonymous with fire (by Greek and Roman poets).

Similar to how a flame arises out of a little spark, Vulcan was born frail and meek, for which reason he was disliked by his mother and she wished to get rid of him, so she angrily threw him out of Olympus. But the marine divinities, Thetis and Eurynome, received him and he dwelt with them for nine years in a grotto, surrounded by Oceanus, where he went to work and made a variety of ornaments. It was, according to some accounts, during this period where he made the golden chair by which he punished his mother for her judgment and abandonment, and from which he would not release her, till he was prevailed upon by Bacchus.

STAR:

Vulcan, the cosmic craftsman, rules this Star. Most qualities of this Star are opposite to the nature of Vulcan. Vulcan loved the Goddess Venus and the qualities that he loved in her are deeply associated with this Star. This is the "star of opportunity". Vulcan reflects the world of fine living and delusions, and people borne here are to overcome superficial things. This is the 14th Star of the zodiac. Vulcan natives are extremely fascinating and always stand apart from the crowd. Extremely well groomed, with their soft eyes and nice body, they exude a charming persona. Vulcan people are intelligent conversationalists. They have artistic flairs, which they use in day-to-day life. Apart from wearing decorative clothing and jewelry, they are great in arts like interior decoration and visual professions. They are brilliant organizers with an eye for details (like the God Vulcan). They also make good architects and jewelry designers. People born in Vulcan can have deep insight. They are also interested in spiritual subjects.

Vulcan is symbolized by a jewel star. Its nature is that of an artist; imagining and designing new forms, ideas, and illusions.

Moon/Sun in:

Vulcan indicates someone with good opportunities in life, very charismatic, charming, and glamorous. They love bright colors, jewelry and beautiful things. They are artistic, spiritual and have great insight, and are good conversationalists and organizers. Judgment is the downfall of Vulcan.

15. FAVONIUS (BUFFALO) October 23rd to November 5th

Sign: 6'40 Libra to 20' Libra

Lord: North Node

God: Favonius

Nature: Angelic

Animal: Buffalo

Body Part: Chest

GOD:

Favonius was the God of the west wind, one of the four directional Anemoi (wind Gods). He was also the God of spring, husband of Khloris (greenery), and father of Karpos (fruit).

Favonius' most famous myth told the story of his rivalry with the God Apollo for the love of Hyakinthos. One day he spied the pair playing a game of quoits in a meadow, and in a jealous rage, struck the disc with a gust of wind, causing it to veer off course and strike the boy in the head, killing him instantly. Apollo, in his grief, transformed the dying boy into a larkspur flower.

Favonius was portrayed in classical art as a handsome, winged youth.

STAR:

This Star is concerned with air, wind, breeze or knowledge of ether (the abode of air). Favonius can be destructive unless one learns how to use the energy of the Star to remove negativity. This Star is related to the Goddess Minerva; therefore, this Star rules all form of learning, music and arts. Favonius people have an artistic flair for communication. It is because of these qualities that they are quite successful financially and business wise. Ruled by the God of Wind, this Star imparts its natives with the qualities of quick change and restlessness. Favonius people also cherish their independence fiercely; these qualities can make them fickle minded and flexible at the same time. They are quick studies by nature and almost always curious to learn new things.

Favonius is typically symbolized by a young plant shoot blown by the wind or a sword. This symbol combines the two motifs. The curved line intersecting the straight line also represents the balancing of contrasting forces. This Star is adaptable, flexible, diplomatic, and temperate. It occurs halfway through the Star cycle, and relates to all crossroads and compromises.

Moon/Sun in:

Favonius indicates someone who is musical, artistic, creative, intuitive and psychic. They have good business and financial skills and are good communicators. They are good learners, knowledgeable, curious and flexible in their approach. They can be vulnerable but are good survivors. However, they can also be impatient, restless and fickle.

16. DINUS (TIGER) November 6th to November 18th

Sign: 20' Libra to 3'20 Scorpio

Lord: Jupiter

God: Mars

Nature: Infernal

Animal: Tiger

Body Part: Breast

GOD:

Mars, the son of Zeus and Juno, was the God of war who gloried in strife, he loved the havoc of the battlefield and delighted in slaughter and extermination; in fact, he presents no benevolent aspect upon human life.

Epic poets, in particular, represent the God of battles as a wild ungovernable warrior, who passes through the armies like a whirlwind, hurling to the ground the brave and cowardly alike; destroying chariots and helmets, and triumphing over the awful desolation which he produces.

In all the myths concerning Mars, his sister Minerva appears in opposition of him, endeavoring by every means in her power to defeat his bloodthirsty designs. Thus she assists the divine hero Diomedes at the siege of Troy, to overcome Mars in battle, and so well does he profit by her timely aid, that he succeeds in wounding the sanguinary war-God, who makes his exit from the field, roaring like ten thousand bulls.

Mars appears to have been an object of aversion to all the Gods of Olympus, except for Venus. As the son of Juno, he had inherited from his mother the strongest feelings of independence and he took delight in upsetting the peaceful course of life which Zeus himself established, he was naturally disliked and even hated by himself.

STAR:

Mars whom represents the powers of heat and battle, rules over Dinus. It has the symbol of a leaf-decked triumphal gate. Mars was known in ancient time as the God of agriculture and spring. A farmer plows and harvests his crop through thick and thin of seasons with single-minded devotion; similarly, the native belonging to this Star work their way to a focused goal. Enduring every obstacle, they manage to reap their fruits of labor. The success produced by these people is long termed, though often it comes later in life. "Everything is fair in love and war" is their motto. As a result, many a time than not, they tend to gain inflictions on the way. This Star advises them to focus around the same determination of purpose to spiritual enlightenment. People born in this Star are also quick witted, artistic, intelligent, pleasant and popular. They are usually very good in communications or jobs that require emotional or physical strength.

The symbol of Dinus combines its traditional symbol of the triumphal arch with its meaning, "Two-Branched". Dinus relates to the concept of single-minded fixation on a goal, and the painful sacrifice required to meeting that goal. It is the incomplete mind which desires completion.

Moon/Sun in:

Dinus indicates a person who is purposeful, goal oriented, ambitious, competitive, opinionated, forceful and determined. They are persistent and patient, but quick witted and intelligent. They are pleasant and popular and are good communicators, but they can also be abrasive. They usually only achieve success later in life and can be jealous and envious of others.

17. URANIA (RABBIT) November 19th to December 1st

Sign: 3'20 Scorpio to 16'40 Scorpio

Lord: Saturn

God: Venus

Nature: Angelic

Animal: Rabbit

Body Part: Stomach

GOD:

Venus was the great Olympian Goddess of beauty, love, pleasure and procreation. She was depicted as a beautiful woman usually accompanied by the winged Godling Eros (love). Her attributes include a dove, apple, scallop shell and mirror. In classical sculpture and fresco she was often depicted nude.

Venus was, according to the popular and poetical notions of the Romans, the Goddess of love and beauty. Some traditions stated that she had sprung from the foam (aphros) of the sea, which had gathered around the mutilated parts of Uranus that had been thrown into the sea by Saturnus, after he had unmanned his father. With the exception of the Homeric hymn regarding Venus, there is no trace of this legend in Homer, and according to him, Venus is the daughter of Zeus and Dione.

In referring to both the Hesiod and the Homeric hymn on Venus, the Goddess after rising from the foam first approached the island of Cythera, and thence went to Cyprus and as she was walking on the sea coast, flowers sprang up under her feet, and Eros and Himeros accompanied her to the assembly of the other great Gods, all of whom were struck with admiration and love when she appeared. Her surpassing beauty made every one desire to have her for a wife.

According to the cosmogonist views of the nature of Venus, she was the personification of the generative powers of nature, and the mother of all living beings. A trace of this notion seems to be inside the scriptures regarding the contest of Typhon with the Gods; Venus metamorphosed herself into a fish, which is considered to possess the greatest generative powers. But to the popular belief of the Greeks and their poetical descriptions, she was the Goddess of love, who excited this passion in the hearts of Gods and men, and by this power, ruled over all living creation.

STAR:

People born under Urania are extremely popular in their friendships. The ability to go along nicely with people, combined with diligence towards their work, makes them highly successful, since they manage to create a sense of balance between their relationships. They are very loving and loyal to their loved ones. They also love variety and travel frequently; or they set up their career in a distant location and far from home. Urania people also have a mystic side.

Urania's symbol is a staff which may be interpreted as a magician's wand or walking stick. Philosophy, devotion, and travel relate to this Star. Urania transforms Dinus's narrow-sighted obsession into a broader vision of reverence and awe.

Moon/Sun in:

Urania indicates someone who has balanced friendships and relationships and is co-operative, loving, popular, and successful. They are good leaders and organizers and are focused on their goals, but they are also good at sharing. They are sensual, and love variety and travel. They are faithful but jealous.

18. PARCA (RABBIT) December 2ⁿᵈ to December 14ᵗʰ

Sign: 16'40 Scorpio to 30' Scorpio

Lord: Mercury

God: Parca

Nature: Infernal

Animal: Rabbit

Body Part: Right Torso

GOD:

The Parca (the Three Fates or Moirae) were the Goddesses of fate who personified the inescapable destiny of human kind. They assigned every person with his/her fate or individual share in the scheme of things. Their name means "Parts", "Shares" or "Allotted Portions". Zeus Moiragetes, the God of fate, was their leader. In the Greek version, Clotho, whose name means "Spinner", spun the thread of life. Lachesis, whose name means "Apportioner of Lots", measured the thread of life. Atropos, whose name means "She Whom Cannot be Turned', cut the thread of life.

At the birth of a human, the Parca spin the thread of his/her future life and direct the consequences of his/her actions according to the counsel of the Gods. As the fate of a human is terminated at death, the Goddesses of fate become the Goddesses of death, Parca Morta. The Parca are independent and wise, housed in a cave where they direct and watch the fate assigned to every being. To the Parca, this is the play of eternal law. Even Zeus, as well as other Gods and man, had to submit to them. They assigned punishment for evil deeds, their proper functions; then all together they directed fate according to the laws of necessity. As Goddesses of death, they appeared together with the Cer and the infernal Erinyes. The Parca were described as ugly old women. They were horrible and stern. Clotho carried a spindle or a roll (the book of fate), Lakhesis a staff which she points to the horoscope on a globe, and Atropos a scroll, a wax tablet, a Sundial, a pair of scales, or a cutting instrument. At other times the three were shown with staffs or scepters, the symbols of dominion, and sometimes even with crowns. At the birth of each man they appeared spinning, measuring, and cutting the thread of life.

STAR:

Parca creates the vibration of a crone, a chief one, or someone or something supremely glorious and superior due to age and experience. Parca gives the karmic pattern in our life through which we have the opportunity to unlock the reservoir of our personal powers, and emerge truly victorious as heroes. Parca people have hidden occult powers. It is also the Star of summoning courage and moving forward in life. Like the eldest member of the family, a Parca born has to take on the responsibility and power of his loved ones, wealth and business. Sometimes, they posses low self-esteem, and tend to seem critical. They can invoke the power of this Star and emerge as wise, experienced and respected as the eldest member of the family.

Parca remembers past life deaths and can have phobias connected to death and dying. Parca being the last Star in Scorpio brings all subconscious fears to the surface. This means there is a tremendous potential to move pass fear.

Parca is usually symbolized by a round amulet or earring, denoting authority. Seniority and expertise are indicated. The three lines connecting the inner and outer circles of this symbol represent the past, the present, and the future.

Moon/Sun in:

Parca indicates a person with a sense of seniority and superiority, who is protective, responsible and a leader of their family. They are wise, psychic, and are courageous and inventive. They may experience financial ups and downs and can be reclusive and secretive. They also enjoy helping the meek and have a psychological and charitable approach to life.

19. HECATE (DOG) December 15th to December 27th

Sign: 0' Sagittarius to 13'20 Sagittarius

Lord: South Node

God: Hecate

Nature: Infernal

Animal: Dog

Body Part: Left Torso

GOD:

Hecate (or Hekate) was the Goddess of magic, witchcraft, the night, Moon, ghosts and necromancy. She was the only child of the Titans, Perses and Asteria; thus received her power over heaven, earth, and sea.

Hecate assisted Ceres in her search for Persephone, guiding her through the night with flaming torches. After the mother-daughter reunion, she became Persephone's minister and companion in Hades.

Hecate was usually depicted in Greek vase paintings as a woman holding twin torches. Sometimes she was dressed in a knee-length maiden's skirt and hunting boots, much like Artemis. In statuary, Hecate was often depicted in triple form as a Goddess of crossroads.

Hecate was identified with a number of other Goddesses, including Artemis and Luna (Moon), the Arkadian Despoine, the sea-Goddess Crataeis, the Goddess of the Taurian Khersonese (of Skythia), the Kolkhian Perseis, and Argive Iphigeneia, the Thracian Goddesses Bendis and Kotys, Euboian Maira (the dog-star), Eleusinian Daeira and the Boiotian Nymphe Herkyna. In Turkey and Chaldian Oracles, she was seen as the Mother Goddess.

STAR:

The symbol of Hecate is a bunch of roots tied together. This Star signifies everything of basic nature, where motion is finite and limited. Hecate indicates the ideas of foundation, from the very bottom. Hecate people are direct, and prefer to start everything from its core. They are lovers of truth, and are ardent researchers. The Star deity is Hecate, the Goddess of magic and destruction, thus this Star can accordingly create many reversals in life. But more often than not, Hecate people with their hard work, shrewdness and ambition, either manage to sidetrack the calamity, or overcome it, emerging as very successful. Hecate is inside the constellation Sagittarius. This is curious to some because Hecate was strongly equated with the constellation Scorpio. The reason for this is due to the "stinger" of the Scorpion falling directly inside this Star in astronomy.

Hecate's symbol is the "Root" or "Center". This Star also includes the spiritual center. The symbol is a stylization of

Hecate's traditional emblem: a bundle of roots. This bundle of roots represents not only Hecate's urge to seek the essential nature of all things, but also the practice of making medicinal herbs.

Moon/Sun in:

Hecate indicates a person who has a passionate desire to get to the truth and is good at investigation and research. They are direct, ardent and truthful and are shrewd and ambitious, but they can feel trapped and bound by circumstances and may, consequently, feel resentment and a sense of betrayal. They can also suffer extreme reversals of fortune due to Hecate's influence.

20. CETO (MONKEY) December 28th to January 09th

Sign: 13'20 Sagittarius to 26'40 Sagittarius

Lord: Venus

God: Ceto

Nature: Human

Animal: Monkey

Body Part: Back

GOD:

Ceto was a marine Goddess who personified the dangers of the sea. She was more specifically a Goddess of whales, large sharks, and sea-monsters (Greek ketea). She consorted with her brother, the sea-God Phorkys, and produced a brood of awful monsters: Ekhidna (the Viper), Skylla (the Crab), Ladon (the Dragon), the Graia (the Grey), and Gorgones (the terrible Ones).

As the mother of Skylla, Ceto was also called Krataiis (Of the Rocks), Lamia (the Shark) and Trienos (Three-Times). Krataiis was also identified or confused with the Goddess Hecate, a divinity whose power extended over the sea. There was also a Krataiis river in the territory of the Brutti, near the Straits of Messina in Italy.

STAR:

Ceto bestows a proud independent and commanding nature. Just like the manner in which water purifies us after taking baths, the natives born in this Star have a constant urge to improve on themselves and situations in life. They keep on winning battles one after another, and hence it makes one "invincible". Their main asset is a huge reservoir of philosophical and emotional depth, through which they take easy command and precedence over others. This Star is known for declaration of wars. Ceto people move towards their goals with awesome fearlessness and aggressiveness. Yet many people born in this Star remain passive, or confused towards their goals in career and education. Once the confusion clears, they become a symbol of strength.

This Star delights in beauty and fearlessness. Its symbol resembles the seashell upon which Venus emerges from the waters of life. It also resembles Ceto's emblem, the fan. The fan has multiple implications. It can be used to fan a fire (to keep passion alive), to cool off (to survive adversity).

Moon/Sun in:

Ceto indicates a person who is proud, independent, and invincible with strong influence and power over others. They are ambitious and fearless, with a strong urge for constant improvement. They have deep emotions and are philosophical, but they can also be confrontational, angry and harshly spoken.

21. NATURA (MONGOOSE) January 10th to January 22nd

Sign: 26'40 Sagittarius to 10' Capricorn

Lord: Sun

God: Natura

Nature: Human

Animal: Mongoose

Body Part: Waist

GOD:

Natura was the primeval Goddess of the origin and ordering of nature. She was similar to the Protogenos Eros (Procreation), Phanes and Thesis (Creation). The primal being of creation was regarded as both male and female.

Orphic Hymn 10 to Natura (Phusis)"To Natura, Fumigation from Aromatics. Natura, all-parent, ancient and divine, o much mechanic mother, art is thine; heavenly, abundant, venerable queen, in every part of thy dominions seen. Untamed, all taming, ever splendid light, all ruling, honored, and supremely bright. Immortal, Protogeneia (First-Born), ever still the same, nocturnal, starry, shining, powerful dame. Thy feet's still traces in a circling course, by thee are turned, with unremitting force. Pure ornament of all the powers divine, finite and infinite alike you shine; to all things common, and in all things known, yet incommunicable and alone. Without a father of thy wondrous frame, thyself the father whence thy essence came; mingling, all-flourishing, supremely wise, and bond connective of the earth and skies. Leader, life-bearing queen, all various named, and for commanding grace and beauty famed. Justice, supreme in might, whose general sway the waters of the restless deep obey. Ethereal, earthly, for the pious glad, sweet to the good, but bitter to the bad: all-wise, all-bounteous, provident, divine, a rich increase of nutriment is thine; and to maturity whatever may spring, you to decay and dissolution bring. Father of all, great nurse, and mother kind, abundant, blessed: mature, impetuous, from whose fertile seeds and plastic hand this changing scene proceeds. All-parent power, in vital impulse seen, eternal, moving, all-sagacious queen. By thee the world, whose parts in rapid flow, like swift descending streams, no respite know, on an eternal hinge, with steady course, is whirled with matchless, unremitting force. Throned on a circling car, thy mighty hand holds and directs the reins of wide command: various thy essence, honored, and the best, of judgment too, the general end and test. Intrepid, fatal, all-subduing dame, life everlasting, fate (*aisa*), breathing flame. Immortal providence, the world is thine, and thou art all things, architect divine. O, blessed Goddess, hear they suppliants' prayer, and make their future life thy constant care; give plenteous seasons and sufficient wealth, and crown our days with lasting peace and health."

STAR:

Natura is introspective and penetrative and is concerned with intensiveness, the results of the latter being more permanent than the former. The native born in its influence are highly virtuous. They have profound stamina, patience and durability. Natura can grant victory to the person seeking its blessings;

therefore, the subjects of this constellation, when proven worthy by their integrity and persistence of the purpose, are granted success in time. The natives are natural leaders, and are highly respected for their virtuous qualities and unbending ethics. They have the power (mostly dormant) to penetrate deep in spirituality, and if they go towards their path properly, this Star can produce invincible spiritual leaders as well.

Natura exemplifies truth, willpower, firmness, and virtue. Its symbol combines a pyramid (representing the crystallization of power), two elephant tusks and the rising Sun (its ruling planet).

Moon/Sun in:

Natura people are enduring, invincible, patient, righteous and responsible. They have great integrity and are sincere, committed to ideals, ambitious and good leaders. They usually have success later in life and have great stamina and constancy, but they can also be rigid and unbending.

22. APOLLO (MONKEY) January 23rd to February 4th

Sign: 10' Capricorn to 23'20 Capricorn

Lord: Moon

God: Apollo

Nature: Human

Animal: Monkey

Body Part: Genitals

GOD:

Apollo was the great Olympian God of prophecy and oracles, healing, music, song and poetry, archery, and the protection of the young. He was depicted as a handsome, beardless youth with long hair and various attributes including a wreath and branch of laurel, bow and quiver, raven, and lyre.

Apollo, though one of the great Gods of Olympus, is represented in some sort of dependence on Zeus, whom is regarded as the source of the powers exercised by his son. The powers ascribed to Apollo are apparently of different kinds, but all are connected with one another, and may be said to be only ramifications of one and the same, as will be seen from the following classification.

Apollo is *the God who punishes and destroys* (oulios) *the wicked and overbearing,* and as such he is described as the God with bow and arrows, the gift of Vulcan. Various epithets given to him in the Homeric poems, such as hekatos, hekaergos, hekêbolos, ekatêbolos, klutotoxos, and argurotoxos, refer to him as the God with his darts hits his object at a distance and does not miss. All sudden deaths of men, whether they were regarded as a punishment or a reward, were believed to be the effect of the arrows of Apollo; and with the same arrows he sent the plague into the camp of the Greeks. Hyginus relates, that four days after his birth, Apollo went to mount Parnassus, and there killed the dragon Python, who had pursued his mother during her wanderings, before she reached Delos. He is also said to have assisted Zeus in his contest with the giants. The circumstance of Apollo being the destroyer of the wicked was believed by some of the ancients to have given rise to his name Apollo, which they connected with apollumi, "to destroy."

STAR:

Apollo enables to link people together by connecting them to their appropriate paths in life. The natives of this Star are all about listening and learning. This constellation signifies eternal quest of knowledge. Apollo people are restless. They constantly involve themselves in conversations, or listening sessions to collect information. A person born under this Sign is either an ardent student, or a well-versed teacher. They can be excellent counselors, owing to their art of listening and giving advice based on their vast knowledge.

Apollo, although the God of the Sun is ruled by the Moon. It relates to listening to others as well as to one's inner voice. This Lunar receptivity is symbolized by a Full Moon supported by a Crescent Moon. The three smaller circles denote the "three uneven footsteps" associated with Apollo. The lines which connect the smaller circles to the larger one evoke the connection between speakers and listeners.

Moon/Sun in:

Apollo indicates good listening and learning and often on a quest for knowledge and information. People born in this Star are intellectual and wise, and make good teachers and counselors and are good at conversation, but they can also be gossipy and restless. They are interested in the past and their heritage and are extensive travelers. They can suffer troubles and disappointment early in life. Sometimes, natives here are also noted for walking with a limp or some other strange gait.

23. MUSES (LION) February 5th to February 18th

Sign: 23'20 Capricorn to 6'40 Aquarius

Lord: Mars

God: Muses

Nature: Infernal

Animal: Lion

Body Part: Anus

GOD:

The Muses were the Goddesses of music, song and dance, and the source of inspiration to poets. They were also Goddesses of knowledge, who remembered all things that had come to pass. Later the Mousai were assigned specific artistic spheres, in Greek tradition they were: Kalliope, epic poetry; Kleio, history; Ourania, astronomy; Thaleia, comedy; Melpomene, tragedy; Polyhymnia, religious hymns; Erato, erotic poetry; Euterpe, lyric poetry; and Terpsikhore, choral song and dance.

In ancient Roman vase paintings, the Muses were depicted as beautiful young women with a variety of musical instruments. In later art, each of the nine were assigned their own distinctive attribute.

The Muses were originally regarded as the nymphs of inspiration and could grant the power to illumine.

STAR:

Muses builds upon the connections of Apollo and makes them more practical. The natives born in this Star are either inheritors of great wealth, or accumulate it during the course of their lifetime. The symbols of this constellation are musical instruments. Accordingly, one can rightly decipher the musical inclination of Muses people. The subjects are natural leaders as well. This Star also provides many of them with fame or at least a good reputation.

Muses is represented by a drum. This bold and confident Star relates to music and dance, as well as to the larger rhythms of life. The shape of this symbol reflects the rhomboid pattern of the stars of this mansion. It is divided into eight triangles, representing the muses who preside over this Star.

Moon/Sun in:

Muses indicates a person who possesses material wealth and property. They enjoy the idea of recognition and are good leaders, but they can be greedy and self absorbed. They are musical and good at dancing and like to travel. They can also experience marital difficulties due to Mars being the Lord of this Star.

24. AEGEON (HORSE) February 19th to March 3rd

Sign: 6'40 Aquarius to 20' Aquarius

Lord: North Node

God: Neptune

Nature: Infernal

Animal: Horse

Body Part: Right Thigh

GOD:

Neptune, the God of the Mediterranean sea, not only was the God of Water, but also the God of the Water element.

He was a son of Cronos and he was accordingly a brother of Zeus, Hades, Juno, Vesta and Ceres, and it was determined by lot that he should rule over the sea.

According to others, he was concealed by Ops after his birth near a flock of lambs and his mother pretended to have given birth to a young horse, which she gave to Cronos to sacrifice. Neptune was also known as "The Earth Shaker" and was responsible for earthquakes, tsunamis and all roughness of the ocean. On a spiritual level, Neptune was known as the God that devoured sin.

Neptune lived in the depth of the sea near Aegae (hence the name Aegeon) in Euboea, where he kept his horses with brazen hoofs and golden manes. With these horses he rode in a chariot over the waves of the sea, which became smooth as he approached, and monsters of the deep ocean recognized him and played around his chariot. In some literatures, Neptune was pulled by his horses, but in other scriptures he was assisted by Amphitrite. Although he generally dwelt in the sea, he also appeared in Olympus in the assembly of the Gods.

Being the ruler of the sea (the Mediterranean), he is described as gathering clouds and calling forth storms, but at the same he has power to grant a successful voyage and save those in danger, and all other marine divinities are subject to him. As the sea surrounds and holds the earth, he is described as the God whom holds the earth (gaiêochos), and has massive power to shake the earth (enosichthôn, kinêtêr gas).

STAR:

This Star is about healing the human condition spiritually and physically. Aegeon is the Star owned by the North Node. This Lunar Mansion is the large group of faint stars in the Water Bearer (Aquarius). As the symbol of the Star indicates, natives born in this Star are natural healers. Apart from medicine and surgery as professions, they are well versed in unconventional methods of curing others as well. The people born in the Star are inclined towards philosophy, astrology, mysticism, metaphysics and psychology. These people are usually very moody. Sometimes they share extraordinary good rapport with people. At other times, they turn reclusive. Their nature often confuses people with rather simplistic thinking. They are good at professions of mathematician, scientific research, accountant, and medicine. They are also known to be highly opinionated, and usually not tolerant of new ideas or opinions of others. They are also extremely stubborn. This may be one of the reasons they often suffer setback in relationships and marriage.

Aegeon is typically denoted by an empty circle. Emanating from the circle are four lightning-bolts, signifying the subtle electrical force present in all things. There are also smaller circles portraying electrons circumnavigating an atomic nucleus. This symbol also resembles a turtle, the carrier of the world, relating to the transpersonal nature of this often eccentric, reclusive, scientific, and mystical Star.

Moon/Sun in:

Aegeon indicates a person who is a good healer, doctor, or astrologer and often is mystical, meditative, philosophical, scientific and a visionary. However, they can also be secretive, reclusive, moody, depressed, opinionated and stubborn.

25. CHIMERA (LION) March 4th to March 15th

Sign: 20' Aquarius to 3'20 Pisces

Lord: Jupiter

God: Chimera

Nature: Human

Animal: Lion

Body Part: Left Thigh

GOD:

Chimera, a fire-breathing monster, which according to the Homeric poems, was of divine origin. She was brought up by Amisodarus, king of Caria, and afterwards created havoc in all the country around and among men. The fore part of her body was that of a lion, the hind part of a dragon, while the middle was of a goat. According to Hesiod, she was a daughter of Typhon and Echidna, and had three heads, one of each of the three animals before mentioned, whence she is called trikephalos or trisômatos. She was killed by Bellerophon, and Virgil placed her together with other monsters at the entrance of Orcus. The origin of this fire-breathing monster must probably be sought for in the volcano named Chimera near Phaselis, in Lycia, or in the volcanic valley near the Cragus, which is described as the scene of the events connected with the Chimera. In some works of art recently discovered in Lycia, several representations of the Chimera were found in the simple form of a lion.

Late classical writers represent the beast as a metaphor for a Lycian volcano.

STAR:

Chimera rises up our spiritual aspiration in life and takes us out of the domain of selfish behavior. This is a transformational Star where people will sacrifice themselves for a higher cause, to make a difference in the world. Chimera is the Star, which inspires the native born in it to reach for higher goals in life. The people born here are extremely idealistic, and very passionate about their cause. They are also usually non-conformists and fairly rebellious. They tend to acquire eccentric qualities, which give them a lot of trouble in their life. They have excellent oratory skills, which they use effectively to spread their convictions.

Chimera is traditionally represented by a man with two faces, symbolizing the moment of death, when one exists both in this world and the next. It is also often denoted by a sword, representing severance. This symbol combines these two motifs.

Moon/Sun in:

Chimera indicates a person who is passionate and transformational, but a little extreme and indulgent. They are idealists and non-conformists and are good influencers of others and they can also be fearful, nervous, cynical and eccentric. Often their life can be full of sadness and problems.

26. PHORCUS (BULL) March 17th to March 30th

Sign: 3'20 Pisces to 16' 40 Pisces

Lord: Saturn

God: Phorcus

Nature: Human

Animal: Bull/Cow

Body Part: Lower Legs

GOD:

Phorcus was an ancient sea God who presided over the hidden dangers of the deep. He and his wife Ceto were also the Gods of all the large creatures which inhabited the depths of the sea. Ceto's name means the "whale" or "sea-monster" and Phorkys' was probably associated with seals (*phokes* in Greek). Their children were dangerous sea-monsters: Skylla (the crab) a monster who devoured passing sailors, Thoosa (the swift) mother of the rock-tossing cyclops Polyphemos, Ladon (strong flowing) a hundred-headed sea-serpent, Echidna (viper) a she-dragon, the Graiai (grey ones) spirits of the sea-foam, and the Gorgones (terrifying ones) whose petrifying gaze probably created the dangerous rocks and reefs of the sea.

Phorkys was depicted in ancient mosaic as a grey-haired, fish-tailed God, with spiky crab-like skin and crab-claw forelegs. His attribute was a torch.

STAR:

Phorcus, the God of the depths of the deep waters, rules Phorcus. Phorcus grants growth and prosperity in a broad way, benefiting the ones close to them. A person born in this Star is a leader, and follows a virtuous path. Phorcus provides the attributes similar to Chimera, but with a milder approach. The people in this Star are simple in conveying their ideals. Generally, the natives are of cheerful disposition, a protective streak about the ones they love. They have self-sacrificing tendencies. They communicate softly, and are very private. They love seclusion, can be devoted to higher consciousness and can have psychic abilities.

Phorcus relates to another aspect of death, in which consciousness sinks deep into the abyss. This Star is associated with the deep unconscious and the life force residing within. Its deity Phorcus "the God of the Depths", depicted here as a serpentine line ascending a vertical axis.

Moon/Sun in:

Phorcus indicates a person with good discipline and speaking and writing skills, who is cheerful, generous, self-sacrificing and very intuitive. They generally have good wealth and inheritance and have a happy home life; but they like solitude and seclusion and can be lazy.

27. HERMAIA (ELEPHANT) March 31st to April 12th

Sign: 16'40 Pisces to 30' 00 Pisces

Lord: Mercury

God: Mercury

Nature: Angelic

Animal: Elephant

Body Part: Ankles

GOD:

Mercury was the great Olympian God of animals, rules and regulations, roads, travel, hospitality, diplomacy, trade, language, writing, persuasion, cunning wiles, athletic contests, gymnasiums, astronomy, and astrology. He was also the personal agent and herald of Zeus, the king of the Gods. Mercury was depicted as either a handsome, athletic, beardless youth, or as an older bearded man. His attributes included the herald's wand or caduceus, winged boots, and sometimes a winged traveler's cap and chlamys cloak.

The idea of his being the herald and messenger of the Gods, of his traveling from place to place and concluding treaties, necessarily implied the notion that he was the promoter of social intercourse and of commerce among men, and that he was friendly towards man. In this capacity he was regarded as the maintainer of peace, and as the God of roads, who protected travelers, and punished those who refused to assist travelers who had mistaken their way.

STAR:

Mercury governs Hermaia. This Star creates abundance through providing proper nourishment. Hermaia indicates a journey, and may in fact represent our final journey from this life to the next, being the last and final Star. The last constellation of all the Stars is Hermaia. This is the Star where the Moon finishes her journey. Hermaia bids the Moon goodbye and assures a safe journey ahead. The same symbolism can be used for people born in this star constellation; they embark from this life to the next with ease and comfort. Ruled by the God Mercury, the subjects of Hermaia are responsible people who take care of others. They nurture and nourish people around them, and are loving and protective. The result is that this Star grants them prosperity, and bids them farewell at the time of their death to reap the karmic rewards in their next life or in the afterlife.

Hermaia, as the final Star, synthesizes and absorbs the mysteries of the previous Star. This knowledge is portrayed here by an all seeing eye. This symbol also contains two fish, representing the Sign of Pisces and the soul's journey after death.

Moon/Sun in:

Hermaia indicates a person who is sweet, caring, responsible and tends to enjoy caring for others. They are sociable and love humanity and society, and are protective and nurturing. They are devoted to loved ones and are spiritual, communicative, artistic and creative. Disappointments in their early life create compassion and forgiveness towards others, consequently, they are most likely to reap karmic rewards in their next life or the afterlife.

YOUR PERSONAL STAR *(Advanced Astrology from this point onward)

Find your rising Sign in Sidereal Astrology (*www.zodiacal.com*, select chart maker), choose sidereal over tropical when creating your chart and select equal House (remember all ancient cultures used the Sidereal Zodiac) and find your Rising Sign degree. The Star planet that rules over your Rising Sign is your personal planet and the Star the planet is located in is your personal Star. Example: Let's say you have a 28 degree rising in Aries, your rising Sign is Vesta, the planet which rules Vesta is the Sun so the Star that the Sun is in is the Personal Star and the House it is in colors the Star.

Your Personal Star is what the native should strive to be or it is what the native will become through experience. If the native does not reach their Personal Star in their present life, they will reincarnate their next life with their past "Personal Star" as their "Moon Star" to make the lesson more active and personal.

1. Dioscuri is 0° - 13°20 Aries and is ruled by South Node
2. Hades is 13°20 - 26°40 Aries, ruled by Venus.
3. Vesta is 26°40 Aries - 10° Taurus, ruled by the Sun.

4. Pasiphae is 10° - 23°20 Taurus, ruled by the Moon
5. Prometheus is 23°20 Taurus - 6°40 Gemini, ruled by Mars
6. Typhon is 6°40 - 20° Gemini, ruled by the North Node

7. Artemis is 20° Gemini - 3°20 Cancer, ruled by Jupiter
8. Zeus is 3°20 - 16°40 Cancer, ruled by Saturn
9. Hydra is 16°40 - 30° Cancer, ruled by Mercury

10. Persephone is 0° - 13°20 Leo, ruled by the South Node
11. Bacchus is 13°20 - 26°40 Leo, ruled by Venus

12. Hymenaeus is 26°40 Leo - 10° Virgo, ruled by the Sun

13. Sol is 10° - 23°20 Virgo, ruled by the Moon
14. Vulcan is 23°20 Virgo - 6°40 Libra, ruled by Mars
15. Favonius is 6°40 - 20° Libra, ruled by the North Node

16. Dinus is 20° Libra - 3°20 Scorpio, ruled by Jupiter
17. Urania is 3°20 - 16°40 Scorpio, ruled by Saturn
18. Parca is 16°40 - 30° Scorpio, ruled by Mercury

19. Hecate is 0° - 13°20 Sagittarius, ruled by the South Node
20. Ceto is 13°20 - 26°40 Sagittarius, ruled by Venus
21. Natura is 26°40 Sagittarius - 10° Capricorn, ruled by the Sun

22. Apollo is 10° - 23°20 Capricorn, ruled by the Moon
23. Muses is 23°20 Capricorn - 6°40 Aquarius, ruled by Mars
24. Aegeon is 6°40 - 20° Aquarius, ruled by the North Node

25. Chimera is 20° Aquarius - 3°20 Pisces, ruled by Jupiter
26. Phorcus is 3°20 - 16°40 Pisces, ruled by Saturn
27. Hermaia is 16°40 - 30° Pisces, ruled by Mercury

Planets in their Exaltation and Debilitation (Planets in their favorite and least favorite Star)

Planet -Exaltation -Debilitation

Sun- Exalted in **Dioscuri** Fallen in **Favonius**
Moon -Exalted in **Pasiphae** Fallen in **Dinus**
Mars- Exalted in **Muses** Fallen in **Hydra**
Mercury -Exalted in **Sol** Fallen in **Phorkys**
Jupiter- Exalted in **Artemis** Fallen in **Natura**
Venus- Exalted in **Hermaia** Fallen in **Vulcan**
Saturn -Exalted **Dinus** Fallen in **Hades**

Health and Stars

When a planet falls into the 6th or 8th House, the Stars the planet rules over are harmed. If a planet falls into the 6th House, they Stars are harmed but capable of being healed. If a planet falls into the 8th House the Stars are destroyed permanently. Example, if Mercury is in the 6th House, Hydra, Parca and Hermaia are harmed, this means that the ears, right side of the torso and the lower legs will have troubles but are capable of healing. If Mercury falls into the 8th House the issues can be permanent. Also if a planet is debilitated, the Star and the part of the body the Star rule become impaired.

Temperament and use of Stars

A) PERMANENT STARS: Pasiphae, Phorcus, Hymenaeus, and Natura

PURPOSE: Permanent nature, house, village, temple, entering in temple rites, religious works, rites for getting peace, propitiation of portents, coronation, sowing of seeds, planting of small garden, starting of vocal music, friendship, sexual works, making and wearing ornaments.

B) ADJUSTABLE STARS: Artemis, Favonius, Apollo, Aegeon, Muses

PURPOSE: Related to motion and movement, riding on a vehicle or horse, opening of shop, walking first time, walking in garden, making jewelry, learning of a trait and sex.

C) VICIOUS STARS: Persephone, Hades, Bacchus, Ceto, Chimera, Vulcan

PURPOSE: Victimizing others, ambush, burning, poisoning, making and using weapons especially related to fire, cheating, deception, wickedness, craftiness, cutting and destroying, controlling of animals, beating and punishing of enemy.

D) BREWED STARS: Dinus, Vesta

PURPOSE: Fire works, burning of sacred fire, using poison, fearsome works, arresting, adulteration, getting loans.

E) LIGHT STARS: Sol, Zeus, and Dioscuri

PURPOSE: Selling, medical knowledge, using and handling of medicines, literature/music/art, making and wearing jewelry, sex.

F) COMFORTABLE STARS: Prometheus, Urania, Hermaia

PURPOSE: Learning music, singing, wearing and making clothes and jewelry, issues related to friends, female company, enjoyments, sexual passions.

G) CURSED STARS: Parca, Typhon, Hydra, and Hecate

PURPOSE: Being the victim, charm or spell causing disease or death, hypnotism, sorcery, ambush, solving crimes, horror, murder, ghosts, issues related to secrecy, backbiting, initiates quarrels, separation, capture, matters related to friendship and breaking thereof, training animals, pleasure, playing games, new clothes and ornaments, singing, visiting cities.

USING STARS IN TRANSIT

(Auspicious and Inauspicious Activities for the **Moon** and **Sun** through Stars. Find dates for the Sun under "The 27 Stars" chapter starting on page 52).

South Node Stars: Dioscuri, Persephone, Hecate

Auspicious

In Dioscuri: Good for all types of beginnings and initiations, especially those involved in learning new things; Laying foundation stones; Communication; Good for all healing, rejuvenation and exercise; Good for improving physical appearance, self improvement on other levels, and age prevention techniques; Good for all activities requiring quickness of thought and action; Equine related activities; Favorable for buying or selling; Traveling; Repairing vehicles or machinery of any kind; Putting on clothes and jewelry; Planting seeds; Learning astrology and other spiritual, occult sciences; Especially good for installing sacred items such as altars, statues, temples etc.; Legal activities; Favorable for taking up a new name.

In Persephone: Ceremonies of all kinds, especially those requiring pomp and grandeur; Marriage ceremonies; Stage and public performances whether it involves music, oratory or drama; Public displays; Coronations and other royal events; Parades; Award ceremonies; Researching one's lineage; Anything involving the past; Historical/classical studies and research; Taking on a new name; Upgrading to higher and better quality in possessions, Jobs, etc.; Undertaking career strategies; Job promotions; Donating elaborate gifts; Studying ancient knowledge; Religious activities of all types especially those involving ancestor worship; Good for settling disputes or other warlike activities; Timely for seeking favors from powerful people, government and other authority figures.

In Hecate: Activities involving getting down to the root of a matter; Gathering together of knowledge, people etc; Singing, oratory and all activities requiring forcefulness and dynamism; Good for administering herbs and medicines; Suitable for planting, gardening and other agricultural activities; Suitable for laying foundations for houses, construction work, buying and selling homes; Good for expressing sexuality; Favorable for adventures; Good for getting even; Favorable for contemplation, self-exploration and self-assertion; Favorable for meditation on death and fierce deities like Hecate or Typhon; Good for initiation into occult realms and study of sciences like astrology.

Inauspicious

In Dioscuri: Unfavorable for marriage; Endings; Activities requiring patience and perseverance; Sexual activity; Not good for emotional activities; Intoxication; Not good for completions.

In Persephone: Not favorable for lending money; Not good for servile, mundane or common activities; Not good for futuristic planning and exploration; Not very conducive for dealing with new technologies.

In Hecate: Does not favor any activity involving balance, tact, diplomacy; Not good for initiations or beginnings pertaining to materialistic matters; Unsuitable for marital ceremony; Unfavorable for borrowing or lending money and financial transactions in general.

Venus Stars: Hades, Bacchus, Ceto

Auspicious

In Hades: All creative activities are favored; Good for severe, cruel, destructive, competitive or warlike activities; Sexual, amorous and procreative activity; Fertility rites and agricultural activities; Beginnings and endings; Gardening; All type of activities which require use of fire; Good for taking care of postponed or neglected activities; Spontaneity; Ascetic activities requiring self-discipline; Fasting and other purification rites; Dealing with children.

In Bacchus: Marriage, sex, romance; Good for dealing with authorities and all kinds of persuasion; Good for clearing out issues in long standing disputes; Good for confronting enemies in a gentle appeasing way; Rest, relaxation and enjoyment; Artistic activities like painting, singing etc.; Good for using charisma or personal power for gaining wanted ends; Good for buying property; Matters related to property and construction in general.

In Ceto: Facing issues which require courage; Taking a strong stance; Confronting enemies and opposition along with reconciliations and forgiveness; Settling debts; Going to war; Inspiring and inciting others into action; Renewal and revitalizing one's energies, goals and actions on the mental, spiritual, emotional or physical planes; Adventures including exploration into nature and sporting activities; Creative pioneering; Traveling over water, visiting water places and activities connected to water; Sailing and other water sports; Confidence boosting strategies; Worshipping female Goddess energies; Showing off; Acts of bravery; Good for equine activities; Artistic performances; Decorating oneself, dressing up; Visiting ancient sites; Spiritual and occult initiations/attainments; Favorable for agricultural activities; Good for marriage and invigorating sexual activity; All activities connected to its professions.

Inauspicious

In Hades: Most unfavorable for travel (relates to traffic jams and accidents); Not good for gentle activities requiring calmness or serenity; Not good for initiations; Better for endings than beginnings.

In Bacchus: Unfavorable for all activities that require letting go of ego; Not good for starting new things; Not good for intellectual activities; Not good for healing or curing diseases; Illnesses which start at this time are hard to overcome.

In Ceto: Unfavorable for activities requiring tact and diplomacy; Not a good time for calm or inner reflection; Not good for endings unless they promise a brighter future or higher step up the ladder; Not good for on-land journeys and often bad for swimming.

Sun Stars: Vesta, Hymenaeus, Natura

<u>Auspicious</u>

In Vesta: Fire worship; Purification rites; Giving up old habits; Making swift changes and sudden endings; Acts requiring initiative, courage, leadership and executive ability; Making important decisions; Military activities and interests; Debating; Standing up for oneself; Cooking; Sewing and embroidery; Cutting; Shaving; All activities involving the use of fire or heat; All mothering and nurturing activities; Good for starting educational ventures; Good for commending new ventures in general; Good for activities requiring a sense of discrimination, honesty and frankness; Drumming and percussion; Most activities are favorable in this Star.

In Hymenaeus: Favorable for sexual activity and marriage; Good for long-lasting clubs, organizations, societies, etc.; Good for dealing with higher authorities; Good for administrative actions of all types; Buying property or entering a new home for the first time; Openings/inauguration ceremonies and swearing-ins; Making promises; Performing sacred ceremonies and rituals; Wearing new clothes and jewelry; Acts of charity; Career related activities; Paternal activities; Good for activities requiring tact and diplomacy.

In Natura: Planning new beginnings; Putting plans into action; Initial plans for any activity; Beginning things anew; Laying foundations; All spiritual/religious activities and rituals; Activities requiring great discernment and correct judgment; All types of business affairs; Signing contracts; Promotions; Dealing with and having authority; Artistic ventures; Marriage; Sexual activity; Entering a new residence; Public, Political or legal matters; One of the best Stars for initiating any kind of activity.

Inauspicious

In Vesta: Socializing; Diplomatic activities; Rest or relaxation; Water based activities.

In Hymenaeus: Unfavorable for endings of all types; Not good for harsh activities like confrontation, retaliation or engaging with enemies; Not good for lending money if you want it returned.

In Natura: Unfavorable for travel; Not good for concluding matters/endings: Generally good for everything except committing unlawful activities; Unethical, rude, impetuous and primitive behavior is not allowed here.

Moon Stars: Pasiphae, Sol, Apollo

Auspicious

In Pasiphae: Extremely favorable for initiating activities; Favorable for farming activities like planting, sowing; Trading and financial dealings of all types; Good for marriage; All healing and self-improvement measures; Nature exploration and traveling in general; Beginning construction; Romance and sexual activity; Putting the material world in order; Purchase of clothes, jewelry, automobiles etc.

In Sol: Good for most activities done under the Sun; Arts and crafts; Activities that stimulate laughter; All types of hobbies especially things like pottery and jewelry making; Planting seeds and gardening in general; Domestic work; Studying sciences and Astrology; Learning languages; All activities requiring hand skills and repetition; Magic tricks; Playing games; All business activities requiring tact and shrewdness; Good for marriage; Buying and selling, especially items like grains, textiles etc.; Great in getting bargains; Dealing with children; Thievery; Holistic treatments of diseases; Travel and change of residence.

In Apollo: Religious rituals and performances; Beginning new ventures; Entering a new house or buying property; Medical actions and remedial measures; Taking preventive measures of all kinds; Listening to advice (listening in general); Social interactions and public involvement; Learning, study of languages and classical traditions; Reading and writing; Music, philosophy and meditation; Good for sexual activity; Making peace; Organizing in general; Making and taking herbs and medicines; Politics; Purchasing new clothes, items and equipment for home or business; Initiations in spiritual learning; Giving and receiving counseling; Important phone calls; Favorable for travel, especially towards its ruling directions; Taking a new name; Humanitarian actions in general; Worship of Apollo or Minerva.

Inauspicious

In Pasiphae: Not unfavorable for any action except those related to death, demolishing and destruction.

In Sol: Planning long term goals and objectives; Sexual activity; Does not support relaxation or inactivity; Unfavorable for all activities requiring executive ability and maturity; Not good for most nighttime activities.

In Apollo: Unfavorable for aggressive, uncertain or risky activities such as lawsuits, wars etc.; Not good for creative activities involving manual work; Not good for lending, making promises, oaths etc.; Not good for putting an end to things like demolishing old structures; Not good for worshipping fierce deities like Hecate or Typhon; Not considered favorable for marriage ceremonies or adopting children.

Mars Stars: Prometheus, Vulcan, Muses

Auspicious

In Prometheus: Generally favorable for all lighthearted activities; Especially good for travel, exploring nature, sightseeing; Sexual activity; All types of artistic work; Healing and rejuvenation practices; Commencing educational ventures;

Excellent for socializing; Changing residence; Good for all activities requiring communication; Good for setting up altars, religious items and performing spiritual initiations; Good for advertising and sales activity; Taking a new name.

In Vulcan: Health and body improvement measures; Buying new clothes and wearing them; Fixing up residences; Home designing; Any activity related to arts and crafts, creative activity in general; Any type of mechanical activities; Good for giving performances; Putting on gemstones and jewelry for the first time; Decorative activities; Good for spiritual practices like visualizations; All issues relating to the opposite sex; Good for collecting herbs and preparing medicines; Good for all activities requiring charisma, elegance and personal charm.

In Muses: Religious rituals and performances; Creative activities in general, especially musical and dancing; Group activities of all kinds; Mega celebratory events involving huge crowds like concerts, opening ceremonies etc.; All activities involving pomp and splendor; Purchasing moveable and immoveable property; Traveling, good for both short and long journeys; All activities requiring aggression and a pro-active attitude; Lending money and all kinds of financial transactions; Meditation and yoga; Gardening; Buying new clothes, gemstones, jewelry etc.; Favorable for treating diseases and commencing educational ventures; Career activities involving fame and recognition; Learning how to use high tech equipment and weapons.

Inauspicious

In Prometheus: Unfavorable for marriage ceremonies, Bad for hard and harsh actions of any kind; Unfavorable for confrontations or making long term important decisions of a serious nature.

In Vulcan: Unfavorable for Marriage; Direct confrontation; Unfavorable for activities which require getting to the root of things; Bad for investigative activities as illusions are strong.

In Muses: Unfavorable for sexual activity or marriage; Activities of a fixed or restrictive character like giving up old habits etc; Not a good time to form new partnerships; Homely activities like cleaning etc; Dealings with people requiring tact, cleverness and gentleness.

North Node Stars: Typhon, Favonius, Aegeon

Auspicious

In Typhon: Only auspicious for activities related to its profession; Favorable for destructive activities like demolishing old buildings; Discarding old and worn-out habits and objects; Good for confronting underlying issues and consistent difficult problems; Good for research and creative activities within its domain; Good for propitiating fierce deities like Typhon and Hecate.

In Favonius: Good for business and trade activities; Recommended for starting any educational venture; Good for learning in general; Social activities and events; Dealing with the public; Financial transactions; All activities which require a calm and flexible approach; Grooming and self adornment; Buying and selling in general; Actions where diplomacy is required; Pursuing arts and sciences.

In Aegeon: Good for signing business deals and contracts, land and housing deals; Education or learning activities; Travel; Water travel; Bike riding; Acquiring new vehicles; Recreational ventures; Meditation and yoga; Sexual activity; Studying astronomy and astrology; Medicine, therapies, rejuvenation and life enhancing activities; Media events; Technological activities.

Inauspicious

In Typhon: Unfavorable for any type of beginning; Unfavorable for marriage, travel, giving and receiving honors, religious ceremonies, etc.

In Favonius: Not good for travel; Fierce or warlike activities; Aggressive behavior does not pay off in this Star.

In Aegeon: Not good for Marriage or beginnings in general; Childbirth; Fertility treatments; Law suits, arguments; Negative or wrathful action; Not beneficial for too much socializing unless it is work related; Not good for financial matters; Not good for buying new clothes or jewelry; Not good for domestic activities.

Jupiter Stars: Artemis, Dinus, Chimera

Auspicious

In Artemis: Traveling and exploring; Making pilgrimages; Taking herbs and all healing activities; Good for starting over again in projects, Relationships etc.; All agricultural and gardening activities; All activities requiring imagination and innovation; Buying cars and homes; Construction; Starting educational activities; Auspicious for marriage; Good for dealing with children; Donations, teaching etc; Good for spiritual activities like fasting, installing altars, meditation and self reflection; Enjoying life's simple pleasures; Very good for worship of the divine Mother Goddess.

In Dinus: Aggressive or warlike activities; Any activity requiring executive ability; Getting things done which require an argumentative approach; Harsh activities in general; Any activity requiring strong mental focus; Working toward one's goals; All types of ceremonies, functions and parties; Awards or decoration ceremonies; Dressing up, ornamentation, decorating oneself; Romance and sexual activity; Performing penance; Making resolutions.

In Chimera: All dangerous, uncertain and risky activities; All activities of a mechanical or technological nature; Holding funeral Services; Putting an end to things; Exploring death issues; Agricultural activities; All activities connected with water like sailing etc.

Inauspicious

In Artemis: Unfavorable for borrowing or lending money; Legal activities or other activities requiring pushiness or conflict.

In Dinus: Not good for travel; Marriage; Initiations of any kind; Activities requiring diplomacy or tact.

In Chimera: Unfavorable for beginning new things or initiations of all kinds; Not good for traveling, sex, marriage and dealing with the government or higher authorities. Most of the actions carried out under its influence often end up causing pain, anxiety, regret, sorrow or extreme difficulty.

Saturn Stars: Zeus, Urania, Phorcus

Auspicious

In Zeus: Excellent for starting new endeavors; Parties, celebrations, artistic and creative activities especially music and dancing; Traveling; Dealing with enemies and seeking legal aid; Financial planning and transactions; Cooking and food preparation; Gardening; Adoption and purchasing pets; All activities related to children; All healing, soothing and nourishing activities in general; Religious or spiritual endeavors like initiations; Enjoys spending time with one's Mother; Good for worshipping Mother Goddess energies; Laying foundation stones and starting construction; Seeking help in general.

In Urania: Group related activities; Research and study with sciences or occult subjects; Meditation; Exploring nature; Secret activities; Favorable for managerial activities requiring on the spot decision making; Good for travel; Immigration and dealing with all foreign affairs; Healing; Spending time with friends; Finances and accounting; Quiet reflection.

In Phorcus: Quiet peaceful activities; Research, meditation, psychic development and astral exploration; Good for making promises, pledges and commitments including marriage; Beginning construction activities - homes, offices etc; Financial dealings; Beginning activities requiring support from others; Artistic ventures; Treatment of diseases; Sexual activity; Entering a new home; Naming children, organizations etc.; Planting and gardening.

Inauspicious

In Zeus: Extremely unfavorable for marriage; Generally unfavorable for arguments, separations and lower actions.

In Urania: Not good for marriage; Not good for activities requiring direct confrontation; Not good for inaugurations or beginnings; Unfavorable for routine, mundane activities.

In Phorcus: Unfavorable for traveling; Litigation; Dealing with enemies; Activities which require quick, swift action in general; Speculation and gambling; Bad for lending money; Not good for extreme physical movement or exertion.

Mercury Stars: Hydra, Parca, Hermaia

Auspicious

In Hydra: All types of activities requiring harsh measures like administering poisons, filing of lawsuits etc; Good for scheming and plotting against enemies; Good for sexual activity; Good for all low risk, short term activities; Good for meditation.

In Parca: Harsh activities; Plotting; Spying; Scheming; Passing judgments; Getting even; Strong opinions in dealing with difficult issues; Taking control; Expressing one's authoritative nature out of a sense of caring; Administrative activities; Policing or monitoring situations; Occult activities; Acting responsibly; Acts of concern, care or protection; Associating with elders, especially giving assistance to the elderly; Taking care of family matters; Occult activities requiring a lot of penance; Holding discussions over serious issues; Grand planning; Acting restrained out of consideration for others; Setting disciplines for oneself.

In Hermaia: Initiating all activities of a positive nature; Business activities and financial dealings; Anything involving exchange of goods; Good for marriage and sexual activity; Religious rituals; All kinds of traveling; Good for dealing with gemstones; Buying cars, homes and other valuable goods; Creative activities like music, drama etc.; Good for kind, charitable and soft activities; Learning, especially spiritual or occult; Healing and treatment of diseases; Rest and relaxation; Good for leisure activities like gardening; Good for completed task at hand.

Inauspicious

In Hydra: Generally unfavorable for all types of beginnings, marriage, buying a home etc; Not good for mediation or spiritual practice of any kind; Good time to stay under the radar; Especially unfavorable for doing business; Bad for borrowing or lending money.

In Parca: Wallowing in depression and resentment or having a hard attitude; Infidelity; Acts of selfishness or self-centricity; Taking advantage of others; Not good for marriage, healing; Oversleeping or physical exertion; Any dealings which require a lot of tact, sensitivity and gentleness; Not good for traveling.

In Hermaia: All activities requiring harshness and boldness should be avoided; Not good for overcoming difficulties, obstructions, enmity or calamities; Not good for negative, sharp actions like surgery; Not good for strenuous activities of any kind like mountain climbing. Note: The last two quarters of this Star should be avoided for beginnings of all kinds.

Stella Astrology

The Goddess Artemis rose from the forest and gave a discourse about the nine personalities of the stars (Stella) to the fairies. In the mist of discourse, she pulled the individual stars from her hair as she explained them in detail.-OV1

Clotho Stella or Birth Star

The Clotho Stella is simply the Star the natal Moon is placed in. It is your Birth Star. It is number 1 in the Table. For purposes of Stella Astrology, the Clotho Stella is also all of the Stars that have the same planetary ruler as your birth Star. For example, if your birth Moon is Chimera, then your planetary ruler is Jupiter. Therefore, Dinus and Artemis are also considered to be your Clotho Stella and any natal planets in these Stellas are said to be conjunct the Moon.

Stella Astrology Graph

No.	Stella Group	Stellas	Effect
1	Clotho	1, 10, 19	Benefic
2	Euthenia	2, 11, 20	Prosperity
3	Ira	3, 12, 21	Obstacles
4	Eupheme	4, 13, 22	Gains
5	Dira	5, 14, 23	Destruction
6	Gratia	6, 15, 24	Success
7	Cer	7, 16, 25	Destruction, Death
8	Pasithea	8, 17, 26	Enjoyment
9	Fortuna	9, 18, 27	Fortune

The Nine Stella Descriptions

Stella 1: This is the Clotho Stella, the Star of the natal Moon including the other two Stars who have the same planetary ruler as the Moon. This Stella relates to the 1st House. Description: beginnings, ideas, body. The Clotho Stella is equivalent to the Ascendant. Planets here have a marked influence upon one's appearance and personality.

Stella 2: Euthenia Stella, the 2nd Star from the Moon and all Stars ruled by that planet. This Stella relates to the 2nd House.

Description: accomplishment, good care of responsibilities, wealth, receptivity.

Stella 3: Ira Stella, the 3rd Star from the Moon and all Stars ruled by that planet. This Stella relates to the 3rd House. Description: hindrance, prevention, death, self-will, hard work, travel, siblings, competition.

Stella 4: Eupheme Stella, the 4th Star from the Moon and all Stars ruled by that planet. This Stella relates to the 4th and 5th Houses. Description: things that create security, property, home, security of progeny and creativity.

Stella 5: Dira Stella, the 5th Star from the Moon and all Stars ruled by that planet. This Stella relates to the 6th House. Description: averted, missed, obstacles, conflict, enemies.

Stella 6: Gratia Stella, the 6th Star from the Moon and all Stars ruled by that planet. This Stella relates to the 7th House. Just as your husband/wife should be your other half and help your life become more efficient, the 6th Stella manifests these specific qualities as well. Description: perfection, unity, love, admiration and harmony.

Stella 7: Cer Stella, the 7th Star from the Moon and all Stars ruled by that planet. This Stella relates to the 8th House. Description: slayer, destroyer, destruction, change.

Stella 8: Pasithea Stella, the 8th Star from the Moon and all Stars ruled by that planet. This Stella relates to the 9th and 10th Houses. Description: friendly, helpful, dutiful, actions, what the person gives to the world.

Stella 9: Fortuna Stella, the 9th Star from the Moon and all Stars ruled by that planet. This Stella relates to the 11th House. Description: useful, high, producing a lot of goodness in life.

As an example, think of the Stellas in this way: if Venus is in the second Star from the Clotho Star (or 11th or 20th), then the person will create and grow wealth in their life through the use of Venusian qualities, such as art, music decoration or comforting. If Venus was in the third Star (Ira), then there would be a lot of competition in relation to the person's love life. If Venus is in the 4th Star from the Clotho Star then the person derives security from art, music, romance, etc; the native will have a beautiful home and love to create beautiful things. Do you get the idea? The 3rd, 5th and 7th Stellas produce challenges and create obstacles and setbacks. The 9th Stella is the best and yields excellent results. The ruler of the 9th Stella, the planetary ruler of the Fortuna Stella and any planets within the 9th Stella will yield extremely beneficial results in its cycles and planets transiting through them are greatly enhanced. The 1st, 2nd, 4th, 6th, and 8th Stellas will also give good effects.

GETTING IN TOUCH WITH THE PLANETARY GODS

SOL (the Sun)

☐ Talisman or Square, of the Sun
(Note: the Talisman is a Western version of a Yantra. Pouring water over them is a traditional means of charging them with planetary energy, especially good when the Talisman is engraved on copper. They can energize medicine, and be energy sources when placed on an altar or seat. These Talismans, engraved on copper or a planetary metal can be used as a pendant perhaps, or fashioned into a ring. They can even be written on paper/parchment in a planetary ink, and placed in a wallet.)

☐ Total value: 45
☐ Planetary symbol: Eight-pointed star
☐ Direction: East
☐ Gemstones: Garnet, ruby. Solar gemstones are not to be worn if any kind of fever or bleeding is present, hypertension, cardiovascular complaint, or infectious

disease, excessive vanity, domineering traits, pride. Settings should be in gold of 14k or more.

☐ Deity: Sol; He is the color of wine and his vehicle is a chariot of 7 Horses. He wears a Ruby crest jewel on his crown. Robed as a mendicant/sage. He is the Creator of the day and the preserver of the World.

☐ Planetary Profile: Confidence, self-esteem, self-respect, strength of will, courage, drive, motivation, independence, success, self-image.

☐ Colors: Red, gold, yellow, orange.

☐ Herbs: Spicy and fiery such as cayenne, black pepper, dried ginger, long pepper, cardamom, saffron, calamus, bayberry, cinnamon.

☐ Oils: Camphor, cinnamon, eucalyptus, saffron.

☐ Hymn: (Latin) O Sol, Animus Vester Vitam Dat, Ego Lucem Mundi Honoro. (English) O Sun, Your Spirit gives Life, I Honor the Light of the Universe.

☐ Lifestyle: the cultivation of independence/courage. The challenge of fears. Light should be brought into all the dark corners of the mind. One should be able to appear in public, alone; as well as be alone comfortably. Initiative, leadership roles. Spending time outdoors in the direct light of the Sun, along with brief but regular periods of Sunbathing. Ritual adoration of the Sun at dawn, noon, and Sunset.

Luna (the Moon)

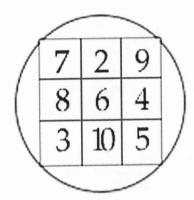

- [ ] Square of Moon
- [ ] Total value: 54
- [ ] Planetary symbol: Crescent
- [ ] Direction: North West
- [ ] Gemstones: cloudy quartz crystal, pearl, Moonstone (use silver setting). Take care when phlegm, edema, congestion, or excessive bodily weight is present, or strong emotions, sentimentality, greed, attachment, excessive involvement with family/society.
- [ ] Deities: Luna; white robed, white lustrous skin, with white ornaments, two armed, holding a lotus in one hand, having a deer as a vehicle, crest ornament being pearl, making the gesture of generosity.

- [ ] Planetary Profile: grounded, emotional stability anxiety, the ability to relate to others, intimacy fears, unfriendliness, weak emotions. Issues of self-contentment, stresses and strains of human contact, moodiness, depression, negativity. Mothers' unhappiness.

- ☐ Colors: white, white shades of other colors, avoiding dark/cloudy colors, or brighter transparent colors.
- ☐ Herbs: Marshmallow, slippery elm, comfrey root, Solomon's seal, jasmine, gardenia, lotus, lily.
- ☐ Oils: sandalwood.
- ☐ Hymn: (Latin) O Luna, Amor Vester Caela Alit, Ego Reginam Noctis Honoro. (English) O Moon, Your Love Nourishes the Heavens, I Honor the Queen of the Night.
- ☐ Lifestyle: atmospheres of peace, faith and devotion, caring and nurturing. Service work. Maternal, supportive, the helping of others, mingling with others, and opening ones heart to the community.

Mavors (Mars)

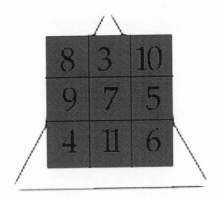

- ☐ Square of Mars
- ☐ Total value: 63
- ☐ Planetary symbol: an upward pointing triangle
- ☐ Direction: South
- ☐ Gemstones: Carnelian, Red coral (use gold or copper setting). Take care using these when the following is present: fever, infection, bleeding, ulceration, excessive sexual drive, anger conflict, argumentativeness, excessive willfulness/impulsiveness, aggression, wrath, martial dispositions.
- ☐ Deities: Mavors; Red robed, red bodied, four arms, being the son of the earth, having a ram for a vehicle, carrying a spear, regarded as the son of Juno.
- ☐ Planetary Profile: issues of energy and motivation, the ability to work, to stand up for one's self. Fearfulness and domination by others. The ability to express anger and to see deeply into the motivations of others. Issues of

passivity, easy control by others, abuse, even physical. Immune system, appetite absorption of nutrients, body weight, muscle strength, liver strength, small intestinal problems, hemorrhoids, bleeding, injuries and the rates of healing in general. Sexual vitality in the male.

☐ Colors: red and fiery colors (darker and more opaque hues). Pure jet black. Avoid grays, browns, blues, greens, and transparent light colors like yellow.

☐ Herbs: many of the herbs of the Sun work here, but in addition: ginseng, astragalus, guggul, myrrh, turmeric, garlic, onions, asafoetida. When Mars is strong, use bitter herbs like aloe, gentian, golden seal, echinacea.

☐ Oils, see herbal section above

☐ Hymn: (Latin) O Mavors, Hasta Vestra Metum Delet, Ego Deum Rubrum Honoro. (English) O Mars, Your Spear Destroys Fear, I Honor the Red God.

☐ Lifestyle: Healthy aggression, daring, activity, expression, physical activities and exercise, discipline in every area, development and pursuit of "Right Goals". This energy should not be applied harshly, but with intelligence and adaptability.

Mercury

- Square of Mercury
- Total value: 72
- Planetary symbol: an arrow
- Direction: North
- Gemstones: Green tourmaline, emerald (gold setting), peridot, jade, green zircon. Avoid the gemstones when wearing gems of the traditional malefic planets (the Indians include the Sun in these), or when the stone has acquired "influences" from previous environments/owners. Otherwise safe and balanced as fits the neutral nature of the Planet.
- Deities: Mercury; Robed in green, the King of wisdom, having a book and sword in his hands. An emerald jewel in his crown, he is peaceful in nature.
- Planetary Profile: Intelligence and/or the lack thereof, communicative abilities, skills, speech defects/virtues,

memory, mental calculations, immaturity (maturity itself might be more purely Saturnian), childishness, foolishness, lack of self-control, addictions, dependencies, slowness of mind, daydreaming, irrationality (the latter few qualities would indicate a weak or debilitated Mercury).

☐ Colors: emeralds, greens, lush natural reflected light from foliage. Avoid reds, oranges, dark colors. Neutral shades, moderate colors, earth tones are harmonious.

☐ Herbs: gotu kola (take care with this), skullcap, passion flower, betony, zizyphus, camomile, mint, sage, basil.

☐ Oils: mint, wintergreen, eucalyptus, cedar, thyme, sage, sandalwood, frangipani, lotus.

☐ Hymn: (Latin) O Mercury, Animus Vestra Silvam Viridem Alit, Ego Deum Sapientiae Honoro. (English) O Mercury, Your Spirit Nourishes the Forest, I Honor the God of Wisdom.

☐ Lifestyle: Reading, studying, thinking. Mathematical and philosophical studies, courses, seminars, school. Greater awareness of the world in general, increasing the powers of communication, the study of a new language, yet always allows time for silence and relaxation in nature as a balance (Virgo). While Mercury rules organization of cognitions, the external world must not rule. Mercury has its proper place in the search for the inner truths of the mind.

Zeus (Jupiter)

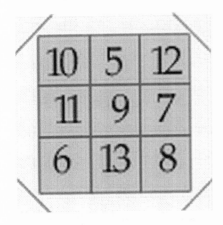

- Square of Jupiter
- Total value:81
- Planetary symbol: Square
- Direction: North East
- Gemstones: citrine, yellow sapphire (gold setting), yellow topaz, yellow zircon.
- Deities: Zeus; Robed in yellow, the King of the Gods, having a bull as a vehicle. His hand is making the gesture of generosity. Yellow sapphire crest jewel. Peaceful in nature.
- Planetary Profile: Joy, enthusiasm, (and the lack of).Weakness of will, of faith. Narrowness, contractedness, meaninglessness, pessimism, depression, anxiety, melancholy, self-pity, may indicate a pathology. Compassion, friendliness, congeniality, material and financial well-being. Creative energies. Childbearing,

vitality, immune functions, healthy (and unhealthy) body fat, liver/pancreatic functions, absorption of nutrients, effective nerve/gland functioning (similar of an overactive Saturn).

- [ ] Colors: yellows, oranges, golds. Clear, bright, transparent colors generally. Avoid reds, blues, violets, purples.
- [ ] Herbs: licorice, ginseng. Nuts such as almonds, walnuts, cashews, sesame seed.
- [ ] Oils: sesame, almond.
- [ ] Hymn: (Latin) O Deus, Animus Vester Tris Mundos Creat, Ego Auro Regem Deum Honoro. (English) O Jupiter, Your Spirit Creates the Three Worlds, I Honor the Gold King of the Gods.
- [ ] Lifestyle: Optimism, faith, high principles (moral and religious), the performance of ritual, the doing of good deeds.

Venus

11	6	13
12	10	8
7	14	9

☐ Square of Venus
☐ Total value: 90
☐ Planetary symbol: a five pointed star (compare numerical placement in a descending planetary series: Saturn, Jupiter, Mars, etc.)
☐ Direction: South East
☐ Gemstones: clear quartz crystal, diamond (settings in gold or white gold), clear zircon. Relatively safe to ware under most circumstances, but can increase sexuality, attachment and the ability for sensory input to over-power the mind. If this is problematic, the higher functions of Venus should be emphasized (devotion, surrender). Avoid when need for luxury is too great.
☐ Deities: Venus; White robed, white lustrous bodied. She is thought of as the teacher of the infernal race, peaceful natured, having a white horse as a vehicle.
☐ Planetary Profile: Beauty, charm, grace, taste, refinement, sensitivity, love, affection, degrees of vulgarity, difficulties with the romantic, feminine qualities in the female, relations with the female gender in the male.

Feelings and expressions. Kidneys, reproductive system, fertility, bone strength, energy, immune functioning, urinary tract complaints.

☐ Colors: All colors, rainbow-like effects. Pastels, light blues, and pinks. Light, variegated colors. Avoid dark, heavy, too bright, too penetrating shades.

☐ Herbs: rose, saffron, jasmine, lotus, lily, iris, aloe gel, amalaki, "dang gui", red raspberry.

☐ Oils: floral scents generally.

☐ Hymn: (Latin) O Venus, Cupiditas Vestra Deos Tenet, Ego Reginam Naturae Honoro. (English) O Venus, Your Passion Rules Over the Gods, I Honor the Queen of Nature.

☐ Lifestyle: A more refined and sensitive approach, appreciative and affectionate. Creativity, artistic endeavor, with the hands, speech and all other modes. Ritual. Dance. Singing. Surrounding oneself with beauty and color. For the female, the free expression of femaleness; for the male, respect for the feminine and the women in one's life, as spouse, as the "beloved", or the high muses of the creative arts.

Saturnus (Saturn)

- Square of Saturn
- Total value: 99
- Planetary symbol: a bow
- Direction: West
- Gemstones: amethyst, blue sapphire (setting in gold), lapis, malachite. To always be worn with care, due to the traditional malefic associations of Saturn (we might adopt a more modern and enlightened view in the West). Best to give the stone a trial run first. Avoid during times of darkness, selfishness, inertia, possessiveness, coldness, or overly crafty natured-ness, pride, manipulation or malice.
- Deities: Planetary; Saturnus is dressed in blue, dark blue bodied, terrifying in appearance yet peaceful in nature, having an ox for a vehicle.

☐ Planetary Profile: Lack of calm, of serenity; agitation, tremors. The ability to handle stress. Insomnia, not grounded. Intimidation by others, or circumstances. Weakness and vulnerability. The practical and the perception of reality. Suffering at the hands of government or organized institutions. The ability to make money. Consistency and the lack thereof, matters of endurance. Long term planning, drive, ambition. Bone and nerve strength, vitality, constipation, tissue decay. Slow healing, resistance to infectious disease. Epilepsy, paralysis, cancer.

☐ Colors: Dark blue, browns, greys, blacks, but care should be taken not to be excessive and emphasize the negative nature of Saturn. Avoid quantities of any hue, especially bright ones.

☐ Herbs: Myrrh, Frankincense, guggal, haritaki, comfrey root- herbs that strengthen and heal the bones. Triphala Churna, a herbal formulation is especially good here, cleansing waste materials, and a tonic for deep tissues generally.

☐ Oils: Sandalwood, frankincense, cedar, juniper, myrrh.

☐ Hymn: (Latin) O Saturnus, Animus Vester Tris Mundos Delet, Ego Patrem Atrum Temporis Honoro. (English) O Saturn, You who Destroy the Three Worlds, I Honor the Dark Father of Time.

☐ Lifestyle: Cultivation of peace, calm and detachment, equanimity, routine, discipline, following authority. Reduction of travel, stimulation of sense and nerve, strong emotions. Spend time in nature and in positive and nurturing environments. Peaceful retreats. Monastic environments.

Caput Draconis (North Node)

13	8	15
14	12	10
9	16	11

- ☐ Square of Caput Draconis
- ☐ Total value:108
- ☐ Planetary symbol: a magnet
- ☐ Direction: South West
- ☐ Gemstones: golden\cinnamon garnet, hessonite (settings can be silver or gold), golden, grossularite garnets. Avoid darker, red or opaque stones, these are associated with North Node's rulership of eclipses. Avoid when natal North Node is in strong associations with malefics, but otherwise relatively safe.
- ☐ Deities: Caput Draconis; He is black robed and black bodied, terrifying in appearance, having a head without a body and the nether regions of a snake, and having a lion as a vehicle.

- Planetary Profile: the predominate influence of our age of materialism. Hypersensitivity, agitation, fear, anxiety, hallucinations, drug consumption, impressionability, moodiness, strange fantasies, imaginings, clouded perceptions. A lack of self-knowledge, leading to impressionability and suggestions from others. Popularity. Unwholesome pursuits, self-dissipation. Immune system functioning, rate of infectious disease spread, pallor, loss of bodily control. Nervous and mental disorders.
- Colors: as in Jupiter as well as the more yellowish of the Solar color range (see above). These counter the negative in North Node and transmit the positive.
- Herbs: aromas that clear the atmosphere subtly like camphor wood, frankincense.
- Oils: scents as above.
- Hymn: (Latin) O Caput Draconis, Vos Caela Devoratis, Ego Regem Insidiarum Honoro. (English) O North Node, You who Devour the Heavens, I Honor the Treacherous King.
- Lifestyle: Most of our modern conditions. Avoidance of powerful sensation, mass media, advertising, anything high tech in general, video/computer games, drugs, too much sex, excess verbiage/conversation and use of the imagination, music videos, web-surfing. The artificial in general should be avoided. Peace, quiet, rest, the pursuit of the authentic, in general; and the cultivation of Jovian things should be helpful. A protective and nurturing environment is essential.

Caudo Draconis (the South Node)

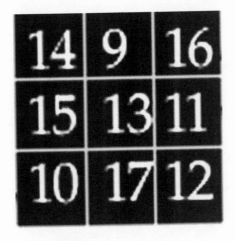

- ☐ Square of Caudo Draconis
- ☐ Total value:117
- ☐ Planetary symbol: a flag
- ☐ Direction: Northwest
- ☐ Gemstones: cat's eye (chysoberyl family), quartz cat's eye (gold settings). Avoid the gemstones during any periods of bleeding, fever, headaches, infections, ulcers, eye pain.
- ☐ Deities: Caudo Draconis; He is smoke colored, grey robed. Two armed, serpent headed, having a serpent as a vehicle, carrying a mace in one hand and the other making the gesture of generosity. Cat's eye crest jewel.
- ☐ Planetary Profile: Insight, discrimination, confidence and the lack thereof. Poor perceptions, or conversely overly acute ones. Self-destructive tendencies. As in an overactive Mars, but more in the nature of a collective

influence from the world around us (a weakened South Node makes us susceptible to injury in war or mass calamities. Sense of constriction, lack of freedom. Excessive attachment to the past, or lost causes. Digestion, circulation, ulceration, anemia, chronic bleeding disorders, muscular problems, nervous disorders with mysterious or unknown causes.

☐ Colors: those of the Sun's range of bright fiery yellows, oranges and reds. Avoid opaque/whitish colors, or the dark and cloudy.

☐ Herbs: subtle, as in North Node. Sage, calamus (use caution), bayberry, wild ginger, juniper.

☐ Oils: camphor, cedar, myrrh, frankincense. Strong South Node types need a bit of soothing with substances like gotu kola, bhringiraj, skullcap and passionflower.

☐ Hymn:(Latin) O Caudo Draconis, Vos in Umbris Equitatis, Ego Regem Temerarium Honoro. (English) South Node, Your who Ride on Ghosts, I Honor the Headless King.

☐ Lifestyle: the developing of confidence in ones thoughts and perceptions. Spiritual and occult studies are helpful. Control and direction of the power of insight. Astrology. Advisable to stick with accepted and legitimate traditions. Discipline, concurrent with the development of will and energy along with compassion and freedom.

Basic Principles of the 12 Solar Houses

Ancient Hellenistic Astrology divides the horoscope into 12 sidereal, equal houses whose positions depend on time and location rather than on date. The houses of the horoscope represent different spheres of life, described in terms of physical surroundings as well as personal life experiences. In delineation the placement of a planet or zodiac sign in a house will determine to a large degree the area of life in which it acts, and the goals and activities on which its drive or impulse will be focused.

1st House (Rising) - Nature of Native, Appearance, Health, Character, Purpose of Life, Behavior, Limbs

2nd House - Wealth, Family, Domestic Comforts, Early Education, Inheritance, Speech Movable Assets

3rd House - Younger Brothers and Sisters, Communication (Talking, Writing, Business Documents), Intelligence, Fine Arts and Music, Short Journeys, Great Prowess (physical and mental), Hands, Arms, Shoulders

4th House - Mother, Emotions, Education, Home, Property and Land, Old Age, Vehicles, Chest

5th House - Children, Lovers, Recreation, Devotion, Speculation and Gambling, Accumulated Karma, Belly

6th House - Diseases, Maternal Uncle, Litigation, Servants, Mental Worries, Enemies, Foreigners, Small Intestine

7th House - Spouse, Business Partner, Death, Respect, Passion, Groin

8th House - Death and Longevity, Obstacles, Suffering, Sexual Organs and Sexual Attractiveness, Occult, Dowry, Inheritance, Imprisonment, Excretory Organs, Accidents

9th House - Father, Luck, Higher Learning, Philosophy and Religion, Mentor or Guru, Prosperity, Travel, Deeds of Virtue

10th House - Profession, Status and Fame, Power, Father, Mother-in-Law, Government, Clothes, Commerce, Knees

11th House - Friends, Hopes, Earnings, Club or Social Activities, Elder Brothers and Sisters, Daughter/Son-in-Law, Calves, Shins and Ankles

12th House - Expenses, Sleep and Convalescence, Sexual Pleasures, Spirituality, Travel and Pilgrimage, Secret Enemies, Imprisonment, Hospitals, Asylums, Liberation, Loss Foreign Residency, Feet

The Lords and Houses

In ancient Hellenistic astrology, each of the twelve Houses of the horoscope is considered to be the same as one of the twelve Signs; in other words, one Sign per one House. That is the ancient Hellenistic system. In modern tropical astrology (Western), there are a number of different House systems employed and most of them are not the equal House system that ancient Hellenistic astrologers use. The equal House, sidereal system has to be employed in this system of astrology. In this way, the Signs in the House are aligned. Example, if you have a 26 degree of Virgo rising then the second House starts at 26 degrees of Libra, making Venus (the Lord of Libra) the second House, Mars (the Lord of Scorpio) the third House etc. Remember, Uranus, Neptune and Hades were not discovered yet. Although I personally use the outer planets, this system works wonders without them.

But in standard Hellenistic astrology, the sidereal equal House system was employed. All of the twelve Signs of the zodiac are ruled by one of the seven planets. The following table shows the ruling planet of each Sign.

Sign	House Lords
Aries	Mars
Taurus	Venus
Gemini	Mercury
Cancer	Moon
Leo	Sun
Virgo	Mercury
Libra	Venus

Scorpio	Mars
Sagittarius	Jupiter
Capricorn	Saturn
Aquarius	Saturn
Pisces	Jupiter

As you can see the Sun and Moon each Lord over one Sign only, Leo and Cancer. Whereas the other planets each have two Signs for which they are the Lord. This is always the case. The Signs never have different Lords. In a horoscope, as mentioned, one Sign is considered the rising Sign and the other Signs follow in natural order, taking control over the other eleven Houses of the horoscope.

For example, if Taurus is the rising Sign, then Venus is the Lord of the first House since Venus is the Lord of Taurus. The second House would then be Gemini and therefore Mercury would then be called "The Lord of the Second." Then Cancer would be in the third House and therefore the Moon would be called "The Lord of the Third."

But the most important thing is to know the twelve Signs very fluently and to therefore know quickly which planets rule each of the twelve Houses for each twelve possible rising Signs. Thus when an astrologer knows the rising Sign, he/she must be able to quickly ascertain in their mind which planet will be the Lord of the ninth House, which planet will be the planet of the fourth House, which planet is the Lord of the eleventh House, and so on.

This process of instantly knowing the Lords of the Houses is very important and fundamental in ancient Hellenistic astrology.

For example, the distance between Sagittarius and Aries is five Signs, because you start counting from the rising Sign. In this case: Sagittarius, Capricorn, Aquarius, Pisces, Aries, that's five. What is the distance between Virgo and Aquarius? Answer is: six Houses. In this way one must be able to quickly know immediately the number of Houses one Sign is away from another Sign. With experience and practice this becomes easy.

Now let us begin to examine the importance and use of the Lords in ancient Hellenistic astrology.

The first House rules over the physique, and can be determined by the first House and it's Lord, aspects upon the first House and the Lord of the first House, as well as planets that reside in the first House, etc. In this chapter we are concerned with the Lords primarily so let us focus on that.

Each Lord must be somewhere in the horoscope; therefore, the Lord of the first House or Sign has to reside in one of the twelve Signs. Lets take the example of Cancer rising. The Moon is the Lord of Cancer. By seeing which Sign the Moon is in we then instantly know what House the Moon is in as well. Let us imagine that the Moon is in Gemini, on a particular horoscope which has Cancer rising. Since Gemini is one Sign before Cancer, this would put the Lord of the first in the twelfth House. Because Cancer is rising, Moon is the Lord, Gemini is therefore the twelfth House and therefore we say "The Lord of the first is in the twelfth".

Primarily, two things happen when a Lord goes to any House. Of these two things, by far the most important to know and understand and be able to read is that the House shapes the Lord that comes to stay in it. For example, the eighth House is a seriously bad House. Of all the Houses in the horoscope, the eighth has the most power to cause bad effects. Therefore, when the Lord of the first House goes to the eighth House in a horoscope, serious physical harm comes to the body. We never like to see the Lord of the first House in the eighth House. Because it means serious difficulty will come to that person during their lifetime.

Again for example, let us say that Taurus is rising. Therefore Venus is the Lord of the first House as well as the sixth House. If Venus is found in the ninth House then the highly benefic affects of the ninth House flow in a great way towards the first and sixth Houses because the ninth House is holding their Lord, passing it's benefic affects onto the first Lord who therefore passes them onto his own Houses. Therefore, to have the Lord of the first in the ninth House which is the most fortunate House in the horoscope, is a very positive Lordship placement.

Since the sixth House is one of the more detrimental Houses because it passes the effects of death, diseases and enemies onto the planets it controls, if the Lord of the first is in the sixth House, these more negative aspects of life will be placed onto the first Lord who will then pass them along to the first House, and all the other Houses he rules (unless he is one of the planets other than the Sun and Moon which rule only one House each).

Now let us briefly examine the main areas of life in which each of the twelve Houses control, and similarly, how this might affect a particular Lord, namely the Lord of the first.

If the Lord of the first is placed in the first House, we would then say the physique becomes the focus of the body. In other words, the person focuses heavily on their own life, their own self and their body throughout their lifetime.

If the Lord of the first is placed in the second House, then the body, first Lord, shall be greatly influenced by and focused upon the things the second House rules such as family and wealth. Thus, those people who have Lord of the first in the second, are found often to be entangled with and coming from a strong family background and they are concerned with accumulating wealth in some way.

If the Lord of the first is placed in the third House, then one's expression is found to be connected with their siblings, the need of college degrees, spiritual initiations and other topics of the third House.

Since the fourth House rules over the mother, home, heart and happiness, if the Lord of the first is placed there then we find the person will be greatly concerned with these affairs during their life. They will likely spend a lot of time at home, since the first Lord rules the physique and the fourth House rules home, we find their body at home rather than on the road or at work etc.

At this point, let us take a small digression into greater complexity and note that since the fourth House is tenth from the seventh House, it would indicate or show the general career of one's spouse/partner. So if the Lord of the first is in the fourth, then we will find it likely that the person's physique will have some connection with the career of the spouse/partner. This means the person might work for or with their spouse and since the fourth also rules over the home, we may expect the person to work from their own home or in perhaps a home-based business.

So the point here is to see that not only does each House rule something when counted from the Ascendant, but it also rules other things depending on its distance from other Houses. In this way the placements of the Lords have their first level meanings and then second, third, fourth and deeper and deeper meanings depending upon the astrologers' ability to read the complexity of the House relationships.

If the Lord of the first is placed in the fifth House, then the concerns of children, creativity, Hellenisticce and what one does to make others happy becomes the focus of their bodily activities to a large degree.

If the Lord of the first is placed in the sixth House, then the affects of death, diseases and enemies overwhelm the person during different times in their life. Understandingly, that is not a good placement for the Lord of the first.

If the Lord of the first is placed in the seventh House, then the person is heavily focused on their partnership, spouse and relationships during their lifespan.

If the Lord of the first is placed in the eighth House, then unforeseen difficulties and serious problems occur throughout life and there is limited physical protection.
If the Lord of the first is placed in the ninth House, then there is an overall fortunate protective cover on the person's body

throughout their lifetime; because the ninth House stands for fortune and all general good things that simply come from the environment.

If the Lord of the first is placed in the tenth House, then the person's body or their life in general is heavily focused upon the attainment of career, status position, and success.

Next the eleventh House controls desires, friends, oldest siblings, and gains. If the Lord of the first is placed in the eleventh House, then the person is heavily focused upon the achievement of desires, relationship with older siblings and the acquisition of wealth.

If the Lord of the first is placed in the twelfth House, since this House rules charity, donations, and losses, the person's body will therefore be used up in these ways throughout their life. In other words they may donate themselves to causes or could potentially live for some other purpose other than their own.

An astrologer must take each of the twelve Lords and examine which House they reside in and predict the affects on each accordingly.

More examples: If the Lord of the second is in the ninth then fortune or wealth will come easily since the ninth is fortune and the second is wealth. If the Lord of the third is in the second, then the younger siblings will have a connection with wealth either by giving or taking.

If the Lord of the ninth is in the eighth, generally this means there is loss to the ninth House, since the eighth is twelfth from the ninth House. Since the ninth House stands for father, it often means the father is absent. And indeed we see this Lordship placement in people who were raised without a father.

If the Lord of the sixth House is placed in the fifth House then there is a draining away of the negative things in life such as death, diseases and enemies. This is good. We do not want the sixth Lord to be strong or prominent. We want him to be weakened because he carries many negative properties.

If the seventh Lord is placed in the ninth House, since the seventh rules spouse and the ninth one's religion, one may find their spouse in their religion. Or their spouse will have an affect upon their religion. Similarly, their religion will have an affect upon their spouse.

When the seventh Lord is placed in the tenth House, we find the person will generally work with their spouse because the tenth is work or career and the seventh is spouse. If the ninth Lord is placed in the fourth, then fortune comes upon their home, heart, etc., (things ruled by the fourth House).

If the tenth Lord is placed in the eighth House, since the tenth rules career and the eighth rules troubles, we find troubles are present in efforts toward career or because of the actual career itself. Most people I know who have the tenth Lord in the eighth House have great difficulty establishing a career. Or when they do establish one, sudden or serious troubles come and greatly harm their progress in their career.

Because the eleventh Lord has much to do with gains and achievement of one's desires, it's placement in the various twelve Houses tells us a lot about how one will attain desires in life and where their desires reside. For example, if the eleventh Lord is in the ninth House, then fortune flows to the achievement of their desires. If the eleventh Lord is in the eighth House, then great trouble will afflict and destroy their desires.

The twelfth Lord rules loss and as we said, the House in which the Lord resides greatly effects that Lord and its Houses. So if the twelfth is in the ninth House then religion, spirituality and God above, have a great affect upon the losses in one's life. What could this mean? It means that losses could come to someone because of their faith, spirituality, or acts of God. There will tend to be losses based upon the person's religion or by situations which are good and righteous but still cause "loss".

So the most important element to a Lord placed in a House, is the House it is placed in, greatly shapes how the Lord will act.

LORDS AND STARS

Because we examined the Lord's different placements in the Houses, we will now take it one step deeper with the Stars. When a Lord of a House falls into "Cursed" or "Viscous" Stars, it is considered to be greatly damaged. Example, let's say that someone has the Lord of the 5th in the 4th, this is traditionally a great placement for parenting, and in ancient Rome, this is considered to be a pleasant placement for a mother or father. But if that Lord happens to fall into Hecate or Hydra (Cursed Stars), parenting would be delayed or denied altogether. You have to look at the House the Lord falls in with the Stars nature in order to come up with a perfect analysis. "Cursed" and "Vicious" Stars have more malefic energy than the 6th, 8th and

12th Houses. On the brighter side, a person can be born with the Lord of the 1st in the 8th and if the Lord is in Zeus, the native will be blessed with the power of the Star along with the higher, mystical qualities of the 8th House.

STAR STRENGTH

If someone is born with a Mars/Saturn conjunction in the 12th House, with Mars fallen in Cancer, it is a very malefic alignment. This means all the Stars ruled by Mars and Saturn are greatly disturbed, and any planet that resides in a Star ruled by Mars or Saturn becomes greatly disturbed as well. The opposite also works. Let's say someone has a Venus/Jupiter conjunction in the 10th House of Pisces. All Stars ruled by Venus and Jupiter become empowered with a positive energy. Any planet that resides inside a Star ruled by Venus or Jupiter receives all the prosperity of this conjunction.

Mark of the Wrathful Goddesses

(These marks are NOT definitive, the whole horoscope has to be judged before making a conclusion. Many more marks will be featured in VOL.II)

Mark of Hecate (Void of Course)

Hecate is the deity that shows up at the moment of pain, suffering, grief, loss, trauma and all difficult transitions. Out of all the forms of the Goddess, Hecate may be the most difficult one to embrace because her work is so utterly human. She is the dark side of the Moon that is involved in all the difficulties a person will have to face, emotional, physical and mental. Hecate has many forms, but her power is in grief, fear, magic, depression, wrath, lust and annihilation. When the Moon or Rising Sign hits the last degree of each Sign and enters the first degree of the following Sign it enters the realm of Hecate (29 degrees to 1 degree of the following Sign), the infernal stage of the Goddess. This can indicate early death, periods of trauma, or intense spiritual awakenings. It is very important to calculate this through the Sidereal Zodiac and not the Tropical, as the Tropical is approximately 23 degrees off the actual constellations. My studies have shown this "Mark of Hecate" is strongest as the Moon or Rising Sign moves through the last degree of Parca and enters the fist degree of Hecate.

Mark of Lucifera (another form of Hecate)

The "Mark of Lucifera" is simple, being born on the New Moon. If the Moon is within 13'20 of the Sun, forward or backward, the Star and the Qualities of the Star are destroyed. Example, if the "Mark of Lucifera" is in Vesta, the native born under this mark will lack fire as opposed to possess the fiery traits of Vesta. If this Mark is in the 8th House, 6th House or 12th House it can prove to be fatal or the life of the individual can be plagued with loss or trauma.

Mark of Medusa

Medusa was one of the three Gorgons "The Awful Ones", the daughters of Ceto (whale), daughter of Gaia and Pontus "The Outer Sea", and her brother Phorcus. Supposedly, she was once said to have been a beautiful maiden, famous for her lovely hair, but then was turned into a hideous monster by the Goddess Minerva. Snakes then replaced her beautiful hair, and her gaze was so awful it would turn men to stone. The hero Perseus killed her on a dare, decapitating her and making off with her head, which he gave to Minerva. Thereafter she wore it on her breastplate (aegis) and it symbolized the storm clouds.

After Medusa's death, the head of Medusa entered the psychic sphere of the North Node and her headless body entered the sphere of the South Node.

The "Mark of Medusa" appears when all planets are hemmed in between the North and South Node (this excludes the outer planets); all planets are on the right or left side of the nodes. This "Mark" can create a heavy, lifelong confusion, a snake like gaze, or a great desire to rule or dictate others. There are various forms of "The Mark of Medusa" some are more positive than others. If the nodes are in Infernal Stars, this alignment is significantly harder, as opposed to in Angelic or Human Stars.

Medusa Rising

When the North Node is in the first House and South Node in the seventh House and the rest of the planets are to the left of this axis, the alignment which arises is the "Medusa Rising". Though this alignment has the power to give windfall gains to the native, it is bad for marital life. Generally natives with this alignment tend to get married later in life.

Medusa in the 2nd

When the North Node occupies the second House and the South Node is in the eighth House, it is called "Medusa in the 2nd". This combination is bad for health. The probability of losses and accidents is high with natives of this combination. This is bad for financial prosperity too. The native is continually worried about an insecure financial standing.

Medusa in the 3rd

When the North Node occupies the third House and the South Node is in the ninth House and the rest of the planets are located to the left of the North Node/South Node axis, "Medusa in the 3rd" is born. The native is burdened with mental confusion in all areas of life.

Medusa in the 4th

When the North Node occupies the fourth House and South Node the tenth, this forms "Medusa in the 4th". Anyone born with this alignment will experience trouble in their work environments and suffer from stress and anxiety as well. Sometimes the native has an illegitimate child, or can be an illegitimate child. However this alignment also has the power of conferring high political success and windfall gains.

Medusa in the 5th

When the North Node occupies the fifth House and the South Node is in the eleventh House, this forms "Medusa in the 5th". The native is worried on account of children. There is difficulty in getting a progeny. If the Moon is also afflicted, there is the possibility of being troubled by spirits. In this case if a native falls ill, the recovery time is slow. The probability of being let down by friends is fairly high in this case.

Medusa in the 6th

This alignment is formed when the North Node is in the sixth House and the South Node is in the twelfth House. The native has many enemies and has problems on account of diseases. However, if this alignment acts beneficially (Angelic Stars), it has the power to confer power and political success.

Medusa in the 7th

When the North Node is in the seventh House and the South Node is in the first House, this forms "Medusa in the 7th". The native has speculative tendencies and can lose wealth by way of wine, sex and gambling. There is marital discord in the life of the native.

Medusa in the 8th

When the North Node occupies the eighth House and the South Node is in the second House, this alignment is formed. The native is short tempered and can attract enemies on account of extreme focus on lower energies. Also, the native generally does not get paternal wealth.

Medusa in the 9th

When the North Node occupies the ninth House and the South Node is in the third House, this alignment is formed. Natives who have this alignment in their chart have many ups and down in life. They have a tendency to lie and be secretive. They are also short tempered.

Medusa in the 10th

This alignment arises when the North Node is in the tenth House and the South Node is in the fourth House. Litigation problems are common is this case. Punishment by law or the government is possible. However if this alignment operates in a beneficial manner then it has the power to confer the highest form of political power, especially in Angelic Stars.

Medusa in the 11th

When the North Node occupies the eleventh House and the South Node the fifth House, this alignment is born. The native has a tendency to wonder aimlessly and is plagued by confusion. Problems or loss arise from children and romance. However, these natives can experience peace in the latter part of life but will lack wisdom.

Medusa in the 12th
When the North Node occupies the twelfth House and the South Node the sixth House, this alignment is formed. The native has problems relating to litigation. They have many enemies and health problems throughout life.

Mark of Persephone

The "Mark of Persephone" takes place when there are no planets in the Sign in front of the Moon or the Sign behind the Moon. Persephone was abducted by Hades and she was forced to live in the realm of isolation. When the Moon is marked by Persephone, feelings of abandonment, isolation and loneliness are present. The native born with this alignment can be very social and even have close friends, yet still feel great isolation. This person could greatly benefit from realizing the spiritual path is the only way to fill the void.

Mark of Atropos

The "Mark of Atropos" takes place when the Lord of the eighth is in a "Cursed Star" (including Hades). The native with this mark is prone to perversion, accidents or early death.

Mark of the Olympic Gods
(These are the main marks, many more will be featured in VOL. II)

Mark of Apollo
The "Mark of Apollo" takes place when the Lord of the 9th House
and the Lord of the 10th House are conjoined under the same Star.
The Star in which this conjunction takes place is greatly
privileged. As an example, if someone has the Lord of the 9th and
10th placed in Hydra, they may become a master communicator.

Mark of Zeus
The "Mark of Zeus" takes place when Jupiter is exalted in the
Cancer side of Artemis. The native is blessed with fame, a

beautiful body and recognition. This is enhanced if Jupiter is in an angle House (the 1st, 4th, 7th or 10th).

Mark of Cupid

The "Mark of Cupid" takes place when the Lord of the 1st House and the Lord of the 7th are conjoined. The native borne under this alignment attracts people throughout life and is never lonely. Although, if this alignment is afflicted by Caput Draconis or located in Hecate or the 8th House, it can indicate promiscuity.

Mark of Eos (Eos was the Goddess whom desired Mortals.)

The "Mark of Eos" takes place when any planet falls into the 10th House while forming "Stella 8", Pasithea Stella from the Moon. The native with this mark will be famous in life and after death. It was believed the person born with this mark was desired by Eos and was given fame as a reward. Although she was not an Olympian, her mark is one of the most fortunate.

Basic Marks

(An angle House is the 1st, 4th, 7th or $10^{th.}$)

- ☐ **Mars Mark:** Mars in its own Sign or in exaltation, and in an angle House- brave, arrogant, the victor. Common among dictators and athletes.

- ☐ **Mercury Mark:** Mercury in its own Sign or in exaltation, and in an angle House- intellectual, learned, rich. Tends to create successful communicators and commentators.

- ☐ **Jupiter Mark:** Jupiter in its own Sign or in exaltation, and in an angle House- religious, very fortunate. Good for high positions in religion, clergyman, and attainable wealth.

☐ **Venus Mark:** Venus in its own Sign or in exaltation, and in an angle House- wealthy, loves life, sometimes self-indulgent, good marriage, strong sense of justice. Good for a millionaire or beauty queens/pagents.

☐ **Saturn Mark:** Saturn in its own Sign or in exaltation, and in an angle House- powerful, strict, position of authority. Good for politicians, yogis or a director.

Counterparts in Asterian Astrology

Match the male's Sun to the female's Moon, example; a male with
a Hades "Male Elephant" Sun would do great with a woman
with a Hermaia "Female Elephant" Moon.

PALACE	GENDER	ANIMAL	COMPATIBLE	INCOMPATIBLE
Dioscuri	Male	Horse	Female Horse	Buffalo
Aidoneus	Male	Elephant	Female Elephant	Lion
Vesta	Female	Ram	Male Ram	Monkey
Pasiphae	Male	Serpent	Female Serpent	Mongoose
Prometheus	Female	Serpent	Male Serpent	Tiger, Dog
Typhon	Female	Dog	Male Dog	Dog, Rat, Mink
Posperos	Female	Cat	Male Cat	Monkey
Jove	Male	Ram	Female Ram	Dog, Rat, Mink
Hydra	Male	Cat	Female Cat	Dog, Rat, Mink
Proserpina	Female	Rat	Mink	Cat
Bacchus	Female	Mink	Rat	Cat
Hymenaeus	Male	Bull	Cow	Tiger
Sol	Female	Buffalo	Male Buffalo	Horse
Vulcan	Female	Tiger	Male Tiger	Cow/Bull
Favonius	Male	Buffalo	Female Buffalo	Horse
Ares	Male	Tiger	Female Tiger	Cow/Bull
Urania	Female	Rabbit	Male Rabbit	Tiger, Dog
Parca	Male	Rabbit	Female Rabbit	Tiger, Dog
Enodia	Male	Dog	Female Dog	Tiger, RABBIT
Ceto	Female	Monkey	Male Monkey	Dog, RAM
Natura	Male	Mongoose	Mink/ Rat	Serpent
Apollo	Male	Monkey	Female Monkey	Dog, RAM
Musa	Female	Lion	Male Lion	Elephant
Aegeon	Female	Horse	Male Horse	Buffalo
Chimera	Male	Lion	Female Lion	Elephant
Phorcys	Female	Cow	Bull	Tiger
Nomius	Female	Elephant	Male Elephant	Lion

Do not be alarmed if you and your partner are not counterparts, this chapter is about mental harmony. Almost all ancient cultures preferred prearranged marriage and this interpretation was used for that purpose. The "starred" qualities are the higher aspect of each person in a relationship.

Dioscuri and Aegeon-The Horse

The Greco-Romans associated the Horse with the spoils of war and attributed it to symbolism such as power, victory, honor, domination and virility. In Greco-Roman myth the Horse is said to be created by Poseidon (Neptune) and is devoted to Hades (Hades) and Dinus (Mars).

Positive relationship and personality traits:

* Power
* Grace
* Beauty
* Nobility
* Strength
* Freedom

Hades and Hermaia-The Elephant

To the Greek way of thought, the elephant represents fortune, luck, protection and is a blessing upon all new projects. The elephant in all his magnificently vibrant glory, is intent on bulldozing through obstacles (oddly enough, male elephants are termed "Bulls").

Positive relationship and personality traits:

* Reliability

* Dignity
* Power
* Royalty
* Pride

Vesta and Zeus-The Ram

The animal symbolism of the ram speaks of great power and fearlessness. A look into mythology will reveal the ram was associated with many gods over time.

The Celtic God Cernnunos is shown with the ram. Some depictions show him seated with a ram-headed snake by his side a symbolic gesture of renewal and power.

In ancient Egypt the god Amun-Ra took on the persona of Khnum, the creator god who was always depicted with a ram's head.

In Rome, Zeus's personality was associated with the ram.

Positive relationship and personality traits:

* Power
* Force
* Drive
* Energy
* Virility
* Protection
* Fearlessness

Pasiphae and Promethues-The Snake

The snake deals with primordial life force and usually turns our attention to gender supremacy (both male and female).

Consequently, snakes span the symbolic bridge between Lunar and Solar associations as well as aspects between water and fire. Coiled within this polarity, we clearly see symbolism of duality and the search for balance.

Positive relationship and personality traits:

* Rebirth
* Patience
* Fertility
* Balance
* Intuition
* Healing
* Protection
* Transformation
* Occult (hidden) Knowledge

Typhon and Hecate-The Dog

The theme of communication becomes heightened when we peer into histories and discover dog meaning and symbolism is connected to the metaphysical realms. The dog has long been considered a liaison between the physical and non-physical dimensions. Ancient Egyptian, Greek, Roman, Celtic traditions have all seen the dog as a sacred guardian of the underworld - those realms outside our daily/mundane experience. If you hear of dogs being symbols of death - this is the connection: Dogs are the guardians of ephemeral domains, and can even serve as spirit guides in non-physical journeys.

Dogs are sacred to Hecate, the Greco/Roman overseer of death, darkness, Astrology, wild wandering, lunar moodiness, midnight journeying and the goddess Hecate defends the soul's right to wander in these little-known, often miSunderstood alleyways. With her highly perceptive hounds guiding the way (and protecting the body as the spirit wanders), astral travel becomes eons easier.

Positive relationship and personality traits:

* Fidelity
* Loyalty
* Assistance
* Intelligence
* Obedience
* Protection
* Community
* Cooperation
* Resourcefulness
* Communication

Artemis and Hydra-The Cat

As an ancient Roman/Greco animal, the cat represents the guardian of the Underworld, depending which texts you read from various regions. Stoic, silent and mysterious, cats fit the bill of Otherworld guardians quite well. They keep the secrets of the Otherworld eternally to themselves, as they gaze with guile upon a world that does not see or understand the depth of their knowledge.

In Ancient Rome the cat was sacred to Artemis, the Moon goddess. Here the cat was also considered a guardian of homes and a symbol of domestic goodness.

In ancient Egypt cats were sacred and were even depicted on the head of their lunar goddess Bastet, which was worshipped by the ancient Egyptians. In her honor, cats were even mummified along with mice for them to eat.

Positive relationship and personality traits:

* Private
* Mysterious
* Intelligent
* Intuitive
* Supernatural
* Watchfulness
* Selective
* Independent

Persephone and Bacchus-Rat/Mink

The mink/rat represents fun and the ability to take life a little less seriously. We can see this in the mink/rat's daily antics in our yards and surroundings. However, other animal symbolism of the mink deals with practicality. As the mink and rat is commonly known to save its food and return to it in the winter months - we take this as a sign in our own lives; a sign that it might be time to look into our own provisions. The mink represents beauty and practicality. Although the mink and rat are a pair, here are their individual traits.

Positive relationship and personality traits of the mink:

* Energy
* Play
* Beauty
* Balance
* Socializing
* Preparation
* Resourcefulness

Positive relationship and personality traits of the rat:

*Industriousness
*Ingenuity
*Necessity
*Resourceful
*Production
*Foresight
*Luck

Hymanaeus and Phorcus-The Bull/Cow

In Roman/Greco mysticism the bull represented physical strength and power. To the Roman way of thought, the bull was also extremely virile, and so symbolized fertility and the power to procreate - to extend the life of the clans. Greeks associated the bull with solar energy and the female cow with earth energy. The bull was also symbolic of great luxury, wealth and provision by later Greeks.

To the Greeks, the bull was an attribute of Zeus (as represented by the constellation of Taurus) who transformed himself into a glistening white bull. Fully tame and quite striking, Zeus (in the guise of the white bull) unassumingly planted himself amongst the herds in an effort to capture the attention of the lovely Europa with whom Zeus was completely smitten. Classic art will show Europa riding a white bull. This is Zeus in the form of a bull, and will touch on symbolism of passion, transformation, virility, strength and fulfillment.

Positive relationship and personality traits:

* Stability
* Virility
* Strength
* Reliability
* Provision
* Peacefulness
* Helpfulness
* Determination

Sol and Favonius- the Buffalo

The Buffalo indicates that you are peaceful, fruitful, practical and generally unaware of your strengths and weaknesses. You are strong, persistent, powerful, tenacious and are unaware of the impact you usually have on others. You are docile and frequently allow yourself to go along with the crowd for self protection and to partake within the social, group. You are a kind nurturing, and giving person. So strong is your respect for life, its goodness and its sacredness that you may fail to set healthy boundaries. In love you are too busy trying to take care of everyone except yourself. You are trying to make everyone happy and may be losing yourself to the collective demands of family, friends, your work, mate and children. Buffalo's can be unpredictable and dangerous when provoked.

Positive relationship and personality traits:

* Provision
* Gratitude
* Abundance
* Consistency
* Strength
* Stability
* Blessing
* Prosperity

Vulcan and Dinus-The Tiger

In ancient Rome this animal symbol was an emblem of dignity, ferocity, sternness, courage, and by itself is power energy. Also a symbol of protection, the image of a tiger is often seen on clothing or in the home to ward off harm any semblance of harm and assure safekeeping. In certain areas of the Mediterranean, the Tiger is regarded as the animal of Wealth. The tiger symbolizes the supremacy of the intangible forces, and our ability to harness power in our lives.

Positive relationship and personality traits:

* Power
* Energy

* Royalty
* Protection
* Generosity
* Illumination
* Unpredictability

Tigers are considered a solar animal which associates them with symbolisms of the Sun, summer and fire.

Urania and Parca-The Rabbit

The Roman believed that rabbits are connected with the Moon and so they run full circle with their cycles. They also share connections of planning and fertility - which are also lunar-based attributes. The rabbit talks to us about conception, conceiving new ideas and holding them in our fertile minds and hearts until they are ready to give birth in their own perfect timing (just as the Moon would have it). And rabbits produce new life in such a humble way. There is no drama, rather there is a quaint, simple, calming way the rabbit goes about offering their new offspring. We can offer our new life (in all its hues) with trust, faith and assurance too.

The rabbit is associated with the Greek Goddess Aphrodite and Roman Artemis. The rabbit is a symbol of efficiency and creative power.

Positive relationship and personality traits:

*Intelligence
*Creativity
*Psychology

*Love
*Friendship
*Planning

Ceto and Apollo-The Monkey

Monkeys are said to possess keen insight in Greek culture and villages portray them as great communicators who posses special insight and clarity. The old adage applied to Monkey's "see no evil, hear no evil, speak no evil" is considered to be the key to right living on earth and these quick and clever animals are seen as the personification of how to live a noble life. Monkeys see dark and light in all things; they weigh all avenues and see things from all angles and possible outcomes.

Monkey's are amiable creatures and enjoy socializing and being with others of their kind. They also exhibit a curiosity for other animals and will often perch high above watching other animals and their habits. At times they will even emulate their actions and movements. Their minds are as quick and agile as their bodies and they are fast learners who display high intelligence.

Positive relationship and personality traits:

* Quick-witted
* Charming
* Lucky
* Adaptable
* Bright
* Versatile,
* Intelligence

Muses and Chimera-The Lion

The fact that the lion is a nocturnal creature means that the lion is a symbol of authority and command over subconscious thought (as night is an ancient symbol of the subconscious - or dream states).

It's interesting that the lion is considered by many ancient cultures to be a solar animal, however it is primarily a nocturnal creature, conducting its hunting activity mostly at night. Further, the lioness is considered a lunar animal.

This serves as a symbolic message of balance and sound judgment. In that the lion shares the world of both night and day, the lion bears a message of prudence to us. The lion has to keep an even mind and an overall balance in our life activities.

In Egypt, the lion represented the ferocious heat of the Sun and was seen in the likeness of Sekhmet who is the Egyptian goddess known as the Eye of Ra. She is the power that protects the good and annihilates the wicked.

In ancient Greece, lions were identified with Dionysus, Phoebus, Cybele, and Artemis because myth indicates lions drew the chariots for these gods and goddesses. Here, the symbolic meaning of lions revolved around protections and they were viewed as guardians of the dead as well as guardians of Stars, doorways, shrines and thrones. They were also ultimate protectors of hearth and home.

Positive relationship and personality traits:

* Courage
* Power
* Royalty
* Dignity
* Authority
* Dominion
* Justice
* Wisdom
* Ferocity

Natura-The Mongoose (Natura is the only one without a pair, suggesting it does best with it's own sign).

The Mongoose, a carnivore related to the civet cat, is of the genus Herpestes. This gray-brown animal lives in India, Africa, and southern Spain. It has a sharp nose, narrow body, and short legs. Its three-foot lenght is about half tail. This creature is easily tamed. Very agile and intelligent, the mongoose is valuable for its destruction of lizards, insects, and snakes, especially cobras. The Mongoose is found throughout the Middle East, including Egypt and India. In some legends listing the weasel, the actual creature meant is the mongoose.

The Mesopotamian goddess Ningilin and the Roman Natura was connected with this animal. The goddess Natura (Nature) was invoked in spells repelling snakes.

Positive relationship and personality traits:

*Defense
*Protection

*Destroying negativity
*Intuition
*Wisdom
*Vision

Simple Chart Interpretations

Due to the complexity of this system, the following interpretations are brief.

Jim Morrison

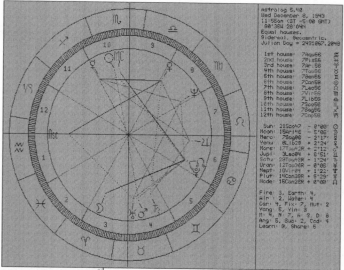

Moon: Hades in 3rd House- The Romans saw the 3rd House as the House of art. This creates a life in the arts with Lord Hades as the Star God. Hades defines Jim Morrison's rebellious nature and his intense focus on death and dying. This would set the tone for his life and nature in general.

Personal Star: Zeus- The rising Sign is under Aegeon which is ruled by the North Node. The North Node falls under the Sign of Zeus. This would signify "Kingship" and recognition. Since the North Node is conjunct Hades, it further explains a connection to death and the possibility of a short life.

<u>Saturn (Lord of 1st) under the "Mark of Hecate"</u>: Short or traumatic life indicated and a personal link to Hecate is revealed through Saturn falling under the 29th degree of Taurus.

<u>MARK OF EOS, Sun in Stella 8, (17 Stars from the Moon) Pasithea Stella</u>: The Sun is under Pasithea Stella in the 10th House, this would show a strong profession and recognition.

<u>Mark of Atropos</u>: Lord of the 8th House Mercury is placed in the "Cursed Star" of Hecate.

(Please note: I believe these forces are always capable of being diverted in other directions.)

Natasha Richardson

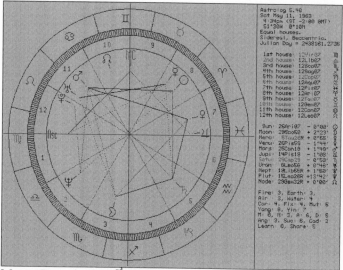

<u>Moon:</u> Parca in the 3rd House shows an artistic person with the Moon in the 3rd. Parca conveys a sweet person with a charitable nature. Helping others in need is an aspect of this Star and the native here will often put others in front of themselves.

<u>Personal Star:</u> Natasha Richardson's personal Star is the Moon's Star, Parca. Her rising Sign is Sol which is ruled over by the Moon.

<u>MARK OF EOS, North Node in Stella 8 in Pasithea Stella (10th House):</u> The North Node

<u>The Mark of Hecate</u> is 29 degrees Scorpio. This degree of Scorpio is the most tragic of all. It is almost certain that the

native of this mark would be forced to deal with trauma, early death or both.

<u>Mark of Atropos</u>: Lord of the 8th House Mars is placed in the "Cursed Star" of Hydra.

Barack Obama

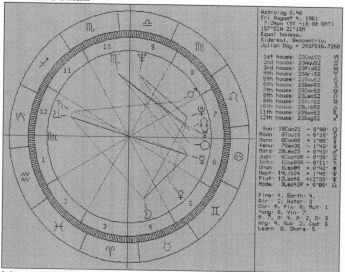

<u>Moon:</u> Pasiphae: People born with this alignment are of sweet-speech, intelligent, capable and bright. Pasiphae has a flair for the fine arts and politics.

<u>Personal Star:</u> Barack Obama has a Muses rising, making Mars his Rising Star planet. Since Mars falls under Hymenaeus, this would indicate he is helpful, kind, friendly, caring, sincere and courageous. Natives here are stable, fixed and focused.

<u>Personal Star in Stella 9 "Fortuna Stella":</u> This generates luck with the 8th House. Strong mystical awareness and fortune with investments from others are positive attributes here. As an example, Barack Obama had a plethora of people invest money into his campaign.

Mark of Hecate: Mars falls under the "Mark of Hecate" in the 8th House. Seemingly, Barack Obama has been through traumatic experiences with the loss of his mother and having little to no connection to his father.

Ted Bundy

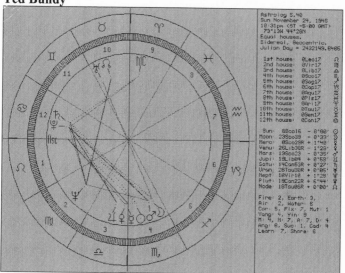

To further prove the superiority of Sidereal over Tropical, I have Ted Bundy who in the Western system has his Sun, Moon and Mars in Sagittarius. In Sidereal, these planets are alive in the Sign of Scorpio. I think most would agree that Scorpio would prove to be the Sign of a murderer.

<u>Moon:</u> Parca indicates a person with a sense of seniority and superiority. The native of this Star may have a connection to psychology as well.

<u>Personal Star:</u> Ted Bundy has a 0 degree Persephone rising, making the South Node his personal planet. His South Node falls into Parca making Parca his Personal Star.

Mark of Hecate: Ted Bundy's rising Sign falls under the "Mark of Hecate" due to it's placement at 0 degrees Leo. The mark of both Hecate and Lucifera creates a short life filled with trauma and a massive amount of anger towards women which would result in severe violence and rage.

Mark of Lucifera: Born the day after an eclipse in Scorpio. To further show the chart of a murderer, Ted Bundy has the "Mark of Lucifera" as well. The Moon/Mars conjunction also explains his extreme animosity towards women. Note that his Moon and Mars just escaped the "Mark of Medusa".

Brittany Smith (working actor and voice over talent)

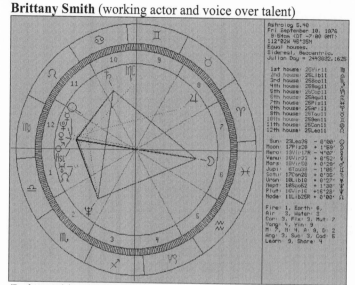

(I chose this chart because if you just look at the 12 Signs, it looks like a difficult chart but when you add the Stars and Marks, you get a different looking and meaning chart).

<u>Moon:</u> The Moon falls under Hermaia. The native here is devoted to loved ones and is spiritual, communicative, artistic and creative.

<u>Personal Star:</u> Brittany Smith is born with Vulcan rising which is ruled by the planet Mars. Her Mars is under the Sign of Sol making Sol her personal Star.

<u>Saturn in Clotho Stella in 10th:</u> This alignment indicates a strong career that would fluctuate due to Saturn also being under the Cursed Star of Hydra.

<u>Mark of Apollo:</u> Brittany Smith has the Mark of Apollo under the Angelic Sign of Sol. The Lord of the 9th and 10th are placed in the same Star. This indicates the ability to be very successful in her chosen field of work.

Planetary Realms and the Seven Planes of Astrological Realization

The false self has to die before the path of the seven planes can begin. As one moves through the Caelums (Heavens), their karma becomes lighter. By the time the aspirant hits the 6th plane, there is nothing left in the aspirant but the love of God. On the 7th Caelum one becomes God! Hecate is the Goddess that removes the veil so the journey back home is possible.

SATURNUS CAELUM (ALM-e-VAKTYA) The First Awakening

After innumerable births of devotion to the path, the mystic enters Saturnus Caelum. The mystic loses consciousness of the earth realm and moves past the astral world. The deity that reflects the mystic's journey appears and reveals the persons individual path. There is no group conscious religion here, only the way that the person will become realized. Swirling circles of light take over the person as they experience the bliss of the deity present. This is the first spiritual enchantment (Samadhi in India). At this stage there is no more evolution, the mystic now enters the stage of involution- the process of unwinding all their impressions to merge into the deity that reflects their highest self.

ZEUS CEALUM (ALM-e-RUHANI) The Realm of Enlightenment

Zeus Caelum is the home to the Elysian Fields where there are fairies, nymphs, satyrs and where the mind manifests the bliss of the hearts desire. When the aspirant enters Zeus Caelum, he/she becomes absorbed in the music of the sirens. The music is so enchanting that the mystic stays absorbed for days. There are 330 million angels on this realm. The Elysian Fields is the resting place for the souls of the heroes and virtuous men. The ancients often distinguished between two such realms-the islands of the blessed and the Lethean Fields of Hades. The first of these, also known as the White Island was an afterlife realm reserved for the heroes and saints of myth. It was an island paradise located in the far western streams of the river Okeanos and ruled over by the Titan King-Kronos or Rhadamanthys, a son of Zeus. The second Elysium was a netherworld realm located in the depths of Hades beyond the river Lethe. Its fields were promised to the initiates of the mysteries who had lived a virtuous life. The Gods of the mysteries associated with the passage of the initiates to Elysium after death include Persephone, Lakkhos (the Eleusinian Hermes or Dionysus), Triptolemos, Hecate, Zagreus (the Orphic Dionysus), Melinoe (the Orphic Hecate) and Makaria. At this stage of the path, the mystic starts to develop mystical powers. All the energies of the Elysian Fields can be manifested in the material world if it is progressive to the individual's journey.

MAVORS CAELUM (ALM-e-KUDASI) The Realm of Zeus

Although all the power of Zeus Caelum belongs to Zeus himself, he sits in Mavors Caelum as King of the World beneath him. When the mystic enters Mavors Caelum, he gains more control over energy and he can now perform major miracles. The eyes of the mystic are swollen and often completely red from the intoxicating power of this realm. Whereas the mystic is intoxicated with the experience and power of angels on the Zeus Caelum, here, on Mavors Caelum, he/she becomes intoxicated with his own energy.

VENUS CAELUM (ALM-e-MAHFAZ) The Realm of Universal Power

When the mystic travels to the fourth plane, he/she has infinite power and can create worlds merely by thought and destroy them as well. This is the home of the shape-shifter and there is no feat that this aspirant cannot achieve. In ancinet Roman/Greco myths, this was the abode of the High mystic. Aphrodite would give this mystic the power to enchant the whole universe. This realm was the most difficult because the person has to be in complete control of their thoughts. If the mystic abused this power, Aphrodite or a Master would turn them to stone and start the whole evolution of the person all over again.

MERCURY CAELUM (ALM-e-ISRAR) The Realm of Pure Knowledge

On Mercury Caelum, the mystic trades in the world of power for divine knowledge. The voice of the Mother is spoken directly to the heart. Mercury (Greek-Hermes/Hindu-Budha) opens the world of divine knowledge. Although the aspirant lets go of power, he is in control of the thoughts of those on Venus Caelum. Here the mystic is completely safe and a friend of God. The music of the sirens on Mercury Caelum is so enchanting that the mystic will stay absorbed for months at a time. The music is the infinite OMNE (OM in Hinduism and Buddhism) and it continually pierces the heart's infinite intelligence.

LUNA CAELUM (PIR) The Realm of Longing

It is here the separation between man and God is so unbearable that the mystic weeps and the tears just flow from the experience of separation of lover and beloved. The Goddess Luna opens the door to the ocean of wine and love and the aspirant is destroyed. Luna Caelum is the home of the Archangels and Luna is their Queen. On Luna Caelum, the person has no karma and their only desire is to unite with the beloved deity. When the person starts to unite with the beloved, Hecate in her highest form as the Black Sun (Nirvan), destroys the last imprint of the aspirant. There is no form in the universe higher than Hecate because there is no form past Hecate. After Hecate, it is the pure attributeless state of Sol Caelum.

SOL CAELUM (ARS-e-MAULA) Unity

Sol Caelum is the merging of the spirit into the ocean of light, the end of reincarnation.

Past Ages (only measured through Precession of the Equinox)

The Age of Leo (The Leonian Age)

Symbol for Leo: ♌

- the vernal equinox (northern hemisphere) is occurring in Leo;

Timeframes

- *Zodiacal 30 degrees*:
  - Common interpretation: ca. 10,500 BC to 8000 BC.

Overview "The Golden Age"
Historical similarities

The major event at this time was an ancient global warming to such a massive extent that it led to the deglaciation of what now constitutes much of the modern habitable world. The deglaciation ultimately caused a 300 foot (90 m) rise in the sea level. The sign Leo is a Fire sign and is traditionally ruled by the Sun in astrology, and it is entirely appropriate that in an Age ruled by the Sun, that the warmth of the Sun melted the glaciers that covered much of North America and Europe. Leo is also related to any kind of light source, and the carved stone oil lamp was invented during this time (Oil lamps existed previously, but this type was the first proper continuously burning lamp.).

The Age of Cancer (The Cancerian Age)

Symbol for Cancer: ♋

The zodiacal signs:

- the vernal equinox (northern hemisphere) is occurring in .
  <u>Cancer</u>;

Timeframes

- *Zodiacal 30 degrees*:
  - Neil Mann interpretation: began in ca. 8600 BC and ended in ca. 6450 BC.
- *Constellation boundary year*:
  - Shephard Simpson interpretation:

Overview "The Age of the Great Mother." Cancer is ruled by the Moon, and is associated with the process of bearing, birthing, nurturing, and protecting.

Historical similarities The <u>Neolithic Revolution</u>, including the beginning of civilization, with <u>domestication</u> of farm animals including pigs, goats and bees. Some nomadic people settled down to living in permanent dwellings. For example, the city of <u>Jericho</u>, believed constructed during this age, was protected by a wall 12–17 ft (4 to 5 m) high & 5 ft (1.5 m) thick. (Cancer is always associated with 'protection' by utilizing an external barrier). There is also evidence of massive loss of coastal regions by the rising sea level following deglaciation of many areas on Earth. This loss of land caused the forced relocation of people to higher ground. Cancer's list of archetypes always include anything to do with the home (including houses, place of residence, migration).

Evidence of widespread use of boats (maritime vessels of all types are ruled by Cancer).

Rise of pottery (a protective vessel conforming to one of Cancer's archetypes).

Religious similarities Widespread evidence of the mother goddess in the Near East (the 'mother' archetype in all shapes and forms is always related to the sign Cancer).

The Age of Gemini (The Geminian Age)

Symbol for Gemini: ♊

The zodiacal signs:

- the vernal equinox (northern hemisphere) is occurring in Gemini;

Timeframes

- *Zodiacal 30 degrees*:

  - Neil Mann interpretation: began in ca. 6450 BC and ended in ca. 4300 BC.

  - *Constellation boundary year*: (not calculated).

    - Shephard Simpson interpretation: (none).

Overview "The Age of Communication, Trade and the Twins"

Historical similarities During this age writing developed, and trade started to accelerate. This corresponds to the symbols the Gemini constellation represents. The constellation can be seen as two people holding hands (thought to be twins), believed by some to be symbolic for trade and communication of peoples. Regardless of the lore associated with the constellation of Gemini, both writing (including literature, newspapers, journals, magazines and works of fiction) and trade (including merchants) are traditional archetypes belonging to the sign of Gemini.

The wheel, although having been used earlier as potter's wheels, was used for the first time for transportation purposes around the 5th millennium BC. Most forms of local transportation (horse and cart, bicycles, suburban trains, trams, cars, motorcycles, walking, roads, freeways etc.) are archetypes associated with the sign of Gemini.

Religious similarities Multiple gods, such as the pantheon of gods in Ancient Greek literature, are believed to have appeared in this Gemini age probably in Sumer (Mesopotamia). (Gemini not only is associated with the archetype of `twins' and `duality' but also 'multiplicity')

The Age of Taurus (The Taurean Age)

Symbol for Taurus: ♉

The zodiacal signs:

- the vernal equinox (northern hemisphere) is occurring in Taurus;

Timeframes

- *Zodiacal 30 degrees*:

    - Neil Mann interpretation: began in ca. 4300 BC and ended in ca. 2150 BC.

- *Constellation boundary year*:

- Shephard Simpson interpretation: began ca. 4525 BC to ca. 1875 BC

Overview "The Age of Earth, Agriculture and the Bull"

Historical similarities Bull worshiping cults began to form in Assyria, Egypt, and Crete which relates to Taurus symbolizing the bull.

Main article: Bull (mythology)

This age is notable for the building of the Pyramids, during the Old Kingdom of Egypt and the Middle Kingdom of Egypt. They personify structure, solidity, stability and attempts at eternity, keywords of Taurus. The completed Great Pyramid of Khufu, clad in smooth pure white limestone, must have been a sight of dazzling beauty in the sunlight. Beauty is another keyword of Taurus.

Taurus is associated with the metal copper, and bronze (an alloy of copper and tin) was for the first time smelted and worked into bronze swords during the early phase of this era.

Papyrus was invented during this time, enabling improved writing techniques. It could be manufactured into very long strips that could be rolled (but not yet folded) into scrolls or rolls for efficient storage and handling. (The Taurus glyph invokes the image of the partially unrolled scroll).

Traits of Taurus such as 'stubbornness' and 'strength' but at the same time 'sensuality' may be attributed to civilizations such as Ancient Egypt's.

Religious similarities

- Ankh: thoracic vertebra of a bull - Egyptian symbol of life

- Worship of Apis, the bull-deity (see also Bull (mythology)), the most important of all the sacred animals in Egypt, said to be instituted during the Second Dynasty of the Early Dynastic Period of Egypt and worshipped in the Memphis region until the New Kingdom (16th century BC).

- When Moses was said to have descended from the mountain with the ten commandments (c. 17th - 13th century BC, the end of the Age of Taurus), some of his people or followers were found by him to be worshipping a golden bull calf. He instructed these false idol-worshippers to be killed. This represents Moses "killing" the bull and ending the Age of Taurus, and ushering in the Age of Aries, which he represents.

- Marduk

- Tauroctony

The Age of Aries (The Arian Age)

Symbol for Aries: ♈

The zodiacal signs:

- the vernal equinox (northern hemisphere) is occurring in Aries;

Timeframes

- *Zodiacal 30 degrees*:
  - Neil Mann interpretation: began in ca. 2150 BC and ended in ca. 1 AD.

- *Constellation boundary year*:

- Shephard Simpson interpretation: began ca. 1875 BC to ca. 100 AD

Overview "The Age of War, Fire and the Ram"
Historical similarities Aries represents a Fire symbol as well as bold actions, a lot of these behaviors can be seen during any age. However, the themes emphasised during this age relate to courage, initiative, war & adventure. Nations during this age such as the expanding empires of China, Persia, Greece and Rome, are often cited as examples of the archetypes of Aries in action. Also the Aries constellation shows a ram running. This could correspond with the sacrifice of Abraham's Ram. While the number of names containing the sound of the ram during this period is noted: Ra (Sun God), Ram, Rama, Brahman, Brahma, Abram/Abraham, Amon Ra, and Ramesses I.The battering ram was employed by the Assyrians, Greeks and Romans with great success during this time. (The symbol of Mars, the planetary ruler of Aries, evokes this interpretation.) According to the Roman state religion, the Roman people were the "Sons of Mars".

Aries is associated with the metal iron, and iron ore was for the first time smelted and worked into iron swords in Anatolia during the early phase of this era, replacing the heavier, softer-metalled, duller-edged bronze swords of the previous Taurus Age.

Traits of Aries such as 'initiative' may suggest the explosion of originality in the development of social aspects, sciences and arts in regions such as Ancient Greece but at the same time traits such as 'Impulsivity' may be attributed to the various Wars of the time.

Religious similarities The Age of Aries ushered in efforts to replace <u>polytheism</u> with <u>monotheism</u>. The earliest known attempt was by the Egyptian Pharaoh <u>Akhenaten</u>, who, in about 1350 BC, decreed the Sun God <u>Aten</u> to be the supreme deity, apparently in reaction to his earlier lack of inclusion in religious rites by his family. After his death, however, power reverted to the original polytheistic priests, who re-established the old religion. Speculation (including that of <u>Freud</u>) has it that later, during the reign of <u>Ramesses II</u>, <u>Moses</u> was influenced by rumour of Akhenaten's revolutionary idea, and grasped the idea of a single supreme God, who especially favoured his people, as an inspirational mechanism that best suited his people held in bondage. The symbol of Aries can be seen as representing the power of multiple gods streaming down into a single god-head.

<u>Moses</u> (born c. 16th–13th Century BC; 7 Adar 2368 - 7 Adar 2488 in the <u>Hebrew calendar</u>), an early <u>Biblical Hebrew</u> religious leader, lawgiver, <u>prophet</u>, and military leader, condemns his own people upon finding them worshiping a 'golden calf' (a symbol of the previous <u>Age of Taurus</u> and of the worship of the <u>bull deity</u>) after coming down <u>Mount Sinai</u>. These events may have occurred during the Age of Aries (see also <u>Dating the Exodus overview</u>).
See also:

- <u>Mithraism</u>

- <u>The Mithraic Question and Precession</u>

The Age of Pisces (The Piscean Age)

Symbol of Pisces: ♓

The zodiacal signs:

- the vernal equinox (northern hemisphere) is occurring in <u>Pisces</u>;

The Age of Pisces is technically the current age and some astrologers believe it will remain so for approximately another 600 years. At that time, the vernal equinox point will no longer be facing Pisces, but moved into the constellation of Aquarius, thus beginning the <u>Age of Aquarius</u>. However, there are many astrologers who believe that the Age of Aquarius has already arrived or will arrive soon.

Timeframes

- *Zodiacal 30 degrees*:

  - Neil Mann interpretation: began in ca. AD 1 and ends in ca. AD 2150.

  - Heindel-Rosicrucian interpretation: began in ca. AD 498 and ends in ca.AD 2654

- *Constellation boundary year*:

  - Shephard Simpson interpretation: began ca. 100/90 BC and ends ca. AD 2680.

Overview

"The Age of Monotheism, Spirituality, and the Fish"

The Origin and History of Astrology

Astrology and the Goddess Asteria

Asteria was the daughter of the titans Coeus and Phoebe and sister of Leto. According to Hesiod, by Perses she had a daughter Hecate.

The Titan goddess of oracles, prophetic dreams, astrology and necromancy, Asteria flung herself into the Aegean Sea in the form of a quail in order to escape the advances of Zeus. She became the island of the same name. Later, the island Asteria was identified with Delos, which was the only piece of earth to give refuge to the fugitive Leto when, pregnant with Zeus's children, she was pursued by vengeful Hera.

The word "Asterism" was taken from the Goddess Asteria.

In astronomy, an asterism is a pattern of stars seen in Earth's night sky. It may form part of an official constellation, or be composed of stars from more than one. Like constellations, asterisms are in most cases composed of stars which, while they are visible in the same general direction, are not physically related, often being at significantly different distances from Earth. The mostly simple shapes and few stars make these patterns easy to identify, and thus particularly useful to those learning to familiarize themselves with the night sky.

The History

The history of astrology in Europe and the Middle East are inextricably linked, with each region contributing to astrological theories and continually influencing each other. Bouché-Leclercq, Cumont and Boll hold that the middle of the 4th century BC is when Babylonian astrology began to firmly enter western culture.

This spread of astrology was coincident with the rise of a scientific phase of astronomy in Babylonia. This may have weakened to some extent the hold that astrology had on the priests and the people. Another factor leading to the decline of the old faith in the Euphrates Valley may have been the advent of the Persians, who brought with them a religion which differed markedly from the Babylonian-Assyrian polytheism.
Babylonia

The history of astrology can be traced back to the earliest phases of Babylonian history, in the third millennium BC.

In Babylonia as well as in Assyria as a direct offshoot of Sumerian culture (or in general the "Mesopotamian" culture), astrology takes its place in the official cult as one of the two chief means at the disposal of the priests (who were called bare or "inspectors") for ascertaining the will and intention of the gods, the other being through the inspection of the liver of the sacrificial animal.

The earliest extant Babylonian astrology text is the Enuma Anu Enlil (literally meaning "When the gods Anu and Enlil..."), dating back to 1600 BC. This text describes astronomical omens and their application to national and political affairs. For example, a segment of the text says: "If in Nisannu the sunrise appears sprinkled with blood, battles." Nisannu is the Babylonian month corresponding to March/April in the Western calendar.

Theory of Divine government

Just as the sacrificial method of divination rested on a well-defined theory – to wit, that the liver was the seat of the soul of the animal and that the deity in accepting the sacrifice identified himself with the animal, whose "soul" was thus placed in complete accord with that of the god and therefore reflected the mind and will of the god – so astrology is sometimes purported to be based on a theory of divine government of the world.

Starting with the view that man's life and happiness are largely dependent upon phenomena in the heavens, that the fertility of the soil is dependent upon the sun shining in the heavens as well as upon the rains that come from heaven; and that, on the other hand, the mischief and damage done by storms and floods (both of which the Euphratean Valley was almost regularly subject to), were to be traced likewise to the heavens – the conclusion was drawn that all the great gods had their seats in the heavens.

Gods and planets

Detail of the Ishtar Gate in Babylon

Of the planets, five were recognized – Jupiter, Venus, Saturn, Mercury and Mars – to name them in the order in which they appear in the older cuneiform literature; in later texts Mercury and Saturn change places.

These five planets were identified with the gods of the Babylonian pantheon as follows:

* Jupiter with Marduk;
* Venus with the goddess Ishtar,
* Saturn with Ninurta (Ninib),
* Mercury with Nabu (Nebo),
* and Mars with Nergal.

The movements of the sun, moon and five planets were regarded as representing the activity of the five gods in question, together with the moon-god Sin and the sun-god Shamash, in preparing the occurrences on earth. If, therefore, one could correctly read and interpret the activity of these powers, one knew what the gods were aiming to bring about.

The influence of Babylonian planetary lore appears also in the assignment of the days of the week to the planets, for example Sunday, assigned to the sun, and Saturday, the day of Saturn.

System of interpretation

The Babylonian priests applied themselves to perfecting an interpretation of the phenomena to be observed in the heavens, and it was natural that the system was extended from the moon, sun and five planets to the stars.

The interpretations themselves were based (as in the case of divination through the liver) chiefly on two factors:

* On the recollection or on written records of what in the past had taken place when the phenomenon or phenomena in question had been observed, and
* Association of ideas – involving sometimes merely a play upon words – in connection with the phenomenon or

phenomena observed.

Thus, if on a certain occasion, the rise of the new moon in a cloudy sky was followed by victory over an enemy or by abundant rain, the sign in question was thus proved to be a favorable one and its recurrence would thenceforth be regarded as a omen for good fortune of some kind to follow. On the other hand, the appearance of the new moon earlier than was expected was regarded as unfavorable, as it was believed that anything appearing prematurely suggested an unfavorable occurrence

In this way a mass of traditional interpretation of all kinds of observed phenomena was gathered, and once gathered became a guide to the priests for all times.

Limitations of early knowledge

Astrology in its earliest stage was marked by three characteristics:

* In the first place, In Babylonia and Assyria the interpretation of the movements and position of the heavenly bodies were centered largely and indeed almost exclusively in the public welfare and the person of the king, because upon his well-being and favor with the gods the fortunes of the country were dependent. The ordinary individual's interests were not in any way involved, and many centuries had to pass beyond the confines of Babylonia and Assyria before that phase is reached, which in medieval and modern astrology is almost exclusively dwelt upon – the individual horoscope.

* In the second place, the astronomical knowledge presupposed and accompanying early Babylonian astrology

was, being of an empirical character, limited and flawed. The theory of the ecliptic as representing the course of the sun through the year, divided among twelve constellations with a measurement of 30° to each division, is of Babylonian origin, as has now been definitely proved; but it does not appear to have been perfected until after the fall of the Babylonian empire in 539 BC. The defectiveness of early Babylonian astronomy may be gathered from the fact that as late as the 6th century BC an error of almost an entire month was made by the Babylonian astronomers in the attempt to determine through calculation the beginning of a certain year. For a long time the rise of any serious study of astronomy did not go beyond what was needed for the purely practical purposes that the priests as "inspectors" of the heavens (as they were also the "inspectors" of the sacrificial livers) had in mind.

* In the third place, we have, probably as early as the days of Khammurabi, i.e. c. 2000 BC, the combination of prominent groups of stars with outlines of pictures fantastically put together, but there is no evidence that prior to 700 BC more than a number of the constellations of our zodiac had become part of the current astronomy.

After the occupation by Alexander the Great in 332BC, Egypt came under Greek rule and influence, and it was in Alexandrian Egypt where horoscopic astrology first appeared. The endeavor to trace the horoscope of the individual from the position of the planets and stars at the time of birth represents the most significant contribution of the Greeks to astrology. This system can be labeled as "horoscopic astrology" because it employed the use of the ascendant, otherwise known as the horoskopos in Greek.

The system was carried to such a degree of perfection that later ages made but few additions of an essential character to the genethlialogy or drawing up of the individual horoscope by the Greek astrologers. Particularly important in the development of horoscopic astrology was the astrologer and astronomer Ptolemy , whose work, the Tetrabiblos laid the basis of the Western astrological tradition. Under the Greeks and Ptolemy in particular, the planets, Houses, and Signs of the zodiac were rationalized and their function set down in a way that has changed little to the present day. Ptolemy's work on astronomy was the basis of Western teachings on the subject for the next 1,300 years.

To the Greek astronomer Hipparchus belongs the credit of the discovery (c. 130 BC) of the theory of the precession of the equinoxes, for a knowledge of which among the Babylonians we find no definite proof.

Babylonia or Chaldea was so identified with astrology that "Chaldaean wisdom" became among Greeks and Romans the synonym of divination through the planets and stars, and it is perhaps not surprising that in the course of time to be known as a "Chaldaean" carried with it frequently the suspicion of charlatanry and of more or less willful deception.

Astrology and the sciences

Astrology played an important part in Medieval medicine; most educated physicians were trained in at least the basics of astrology to use in their practice.

Partly in further development of views unfolded in Babylonia, but chiefly under Greek influences, the scope of astrology was enlarged until it was brought into connection with practically all of the known sciences: botany, chemistry, zoology, mineralogy, anatomy and medicine. Colours, metals, stones, plants, drugs and animal life of all kinds were each associated with one or another of the planets and placed under their rulership.

By this process of combination, the entire realm of the natural sciences was translated into the language of astrology with the purpose of seeing in all phenomena signs indicative of what the future had in store.

The fate of the individual led to the association of the planets with parts of the body and so with Medical astrology. .

From the planets the same association of ideas was applied to the constellations of the zodiac . The zodiac came to be regarded as the prototype of the human body, the different parts of which all had their corresponding section in the zodiac itself. The head was placed in the first sign of the zodiac, Aries, the Ram; and the feet in the last sign, Pisces, the Fishes. Between these two extremes the other parts and organs of the body were distributed among the remaining signs of the zodiac. In later phases of astrology the signs of the zodiac are sometimes placed on a par with the planets themselves, so far as their importance for the individual horoscope is concerned.

With human anatomy thus connected with the planets, with constellations, and with single stars, medicine became an integral part of astrology. Diseases and disturbances of the ordinary functions of the organs were attributed to the influences of planets, constellations and stars.

Arab and Persian Astrology

The system was taken up almost in its entirety by the Arab astrologers. From their great centres of learning in Damascus and Baghdad they revived the learning of the ancient Greeks in Islamic astronomy, astrology, Islamic mathematics and Islamic medicine which Europe had forgotten and developed it. Their knowledge was then imported into Europe, during and after the Latin translations of the 12th century, helping to start the Renaissance. Albumasur was the greatest of the Arab astrologers, whose work 'Introductorium in Astronomiam' was later highly influential in Europe. Also important was Al Khwarizmi , the Persian mathematician, astronomer, astrologer and geographer, who is considered to be the father of algebra and the algorithm. The Arabs greatly increased the knowledge of astronomy, naming many of the stars for the first time, such as Aldebaran, Altair, Betelgeuse, Rigel and Vega. In astrology they discovered a system still known as Arabic parts , which accorded a significance to the difference or "part" between the ascendant and each planet.

The study of astrology was refuted by several medieval Muslim astronomers such as Al-Farabi (Alpharabius), Ibn al-Haytham (Alhazen), Avicenna, Abu Rayhan al-Biruni and Averroes. Their reasons for refuting astrology were often due to both scientific (the methods used by astrologers being conjectural rather than empirical) and religious (conflicts with orthodox Islamic scholars) reasons.

Ibn Qayyim Al-Jawziyya (1292–1350), in his Miftah Dar al-SaCadah, used empirical narguments in astronomy in order to refute the practice of astrology and divination. He recognized that the stars are much larger than the planets, and thus argued:

"And if you astrologers answer that it is precisely because of this distance and smallness that their influences are negligible, then why is it that you claim a great influence for the smallest heavenly body, Mercury? Why is it that you have given an influence to al-Ra's and al-Dhanab, which are two imaginary points [ascending and descending nodes]?"

Al-Jawziyya also recognized the Milky Way galaxy as "a myriad of tiny stars packed together in the sphere of the fixed stars" and thus argued that "it is certainly impossible to have knowledge of their influences.

Astrology in Medieval and Renaissance Europe

Astrology became embodied in the Kabbalistic lore of Jews and Christians, and came to be the substance of the astrology of the Middle Ages. In time this would lead to Church prelates and Protestant princes using the services of astrologers. This system was referred to as "judicial astrology", and its practitioners believed that the position of heavenly bodies influenced the affairs of mankind. It was placed on a similar footing of equality and esteem with "natural astrology", the latter name for the study of the motions and phenomena of the heavenly bodies and their effect on the weather.

During the Middle Ages astrologers were called mathematici. Historically the term mathematicus was used to denote a person proficient in astrology, astronomy, and mathematics. Inasmuch as some practice of medicine was based to some extent on astrology, physicians learned some mathematics and astrology.

In the 13th century, Johannes de Sacrobosco (c. 1195–1256) and Guido Bonatti from Forlì (Italy) were the most famous astronomers and astrologers in Great Britain (the first) and in Europe (the second): the book Liber Astronomicus by Bonatti was reputed "the most important astrological work produced in Latin in the 13th century" (Lynn Thorndike).

Jerome Cardan (1501–76) hated Martin Luther, and so changed his birthday in order to give him an unfavorable horoscope. In Cardan's times, as in those of Augustus, it was a common practice for men to conceal the day and hour of their birth, till, like Augustus, they found a complaisant astrologer.

During the Renaissance, a form of "scientific astrology" evolved in which court astrologers would complieent their use of horoscopes with genuine discoveries about the nature of the universe. Many individuals now credited with having overturned the old astrological order, such as Galileo Galilei, Tycho Brahe and Johannes Kepler, were themselves practising astrologers.

But, as a general rule, medieval and Renaissance astrologers did not give themselves the trouble of reading the stars, but contented themselves with telling fortunes by faces. They practised chiromancy (also known as palmistry), and relied on afterwards drawing a horoscope to suit.

As physiognomists (see physiognomy) their talent was undoubted, and according to Lucilio Vanini there was no need to mount to the house-top to cast a nativity. "Yes," he says, "I can read his face; by his hair and his forehead it is easy to guess that the sun at his birth was in the sign of Libra and near Venus.

Nay, his complexion shows that Venus touches Libra. By the rules of astrology he could not lie."

Astrology in India

The earliest use of the term Jyotisha is in the sense of a Vedanga, an auxiliary discipline of Vedic religion. The only work of this class to have survived is the Vedanga Jyotisha, which contains rules for tracking the motions of the sun and the moon in the context of a five-year intercalation cycle. The date of this work is uncertain, as its late style of language and composition, consistent with the last centuries BCE, albeit pre-Mauryan, conflicts with some internal evidence of a much earlier date in the second millennium BCE.

The documented history of Jyotish in the subsequent newer sense of modern horoscopic astrology is associated with the interaction of Indian and Hellenistic cultures in the Indo-Greek period. Greek became a lingua franca of the Indus valley region following the military conquests of Alexander the Great and the Bactrian Greeks. The oldest surviving treatises, such as the Yavanajataka or the Brihat-Samhita, date to the early centuries CE. The oldest astrological treatise in Sanskrit is the Yavanajataka ("Sayings of the Greeks"), a versification by Sphujidhvaja in 269/270 CE of a now lost translation of a Greek treatise by Yavanesvara during the 2nd century CE under the patronage of the Western Satrap Saka king Rudradaman I.

Indian astronomy and astrology developed together. The first named authors writing treatises on astronomy are from the 5th century CE, the date when the classical period of Indian astronomy can be said to begin. Besides the theories of

Aryabhata in the Aryabhatiya and the lost Arya-siddhānta, there is the Pancha-Siddhāntika of Varahamihira.

Astrology in China and East Asia

The tradition usually called 'Chinese Astrology', by Westerners is in fact not only used by the Chinese, but has a long history in other East Asian countries such as Japan, Thailand and Vietnam.

Chinese Astrology

Astrology is believed to have originated in China about the 3rd millennium BC. Astrology was always traditionally regarded very highly in China, and indeed Confucius is said to have treated astrology with respect saying: "Heaven sends down its good or evil symbols and wise men act accordingly".The 60 year cycle combining the five elements with the twelve animal signs of the zodiac has been documented in China since at least the time of the Shang (Shing or Yin) dynasty (ca 1766 BC – ca 1050 BC). Oracles bones have been found dating from that period with the date according to the 60 year cycle inscribed on them, along with the name of the diviner and the topic being divined about. One of the most famous astrologers in China was Tsou Yen who lived in around 300 BC, and who wrote: "When some new dynasty is going to arise, heaven exhibits auspicious signs for the people". Astrology in China also became combined with the Chinese form of geomancy known as Feng shui .

Astrology in MesoAmerica

The calendars of Pre-Columbian MesoAmerica are based upon

a system which had been in common use throughout the region, dating back to at least the 6th century BCE. The earliest calendars were employed by peoples such as the Zapotecs and Olmecs, and later by such peoples as the Maya , Mixtec and Aztecs. Although the Mesoamerican calendar did not originate with the Maya, their subsequent extensions and refinements to it were the most sophisticated. Along with those of the Aztecs, the Maya calendars are the best-documented and most completely understood.

Mayan Astrology

The distinctive Mayan calendar and Mayan astrology have been in use in Meso-America from at least the 6th century BCE. There were two main calendars, one plotting the solar year of 360 days, which governed the planting of crops and other domestic matters; the other called the Tzolkin of 260 days, which governed ritual use. Each was linked to an elaborate astrological system to cover every facet of life. On the fifth day after the birth of a boy, the Mayan astrologer-priests would cast his horoscope to see what his profession was to be: soldier, priest, civil servant or sacrificial victim. A 584 day Venus cycle was also maintained, which tracked the appearance and conjunctions of Venus. Venus was seen as a generally inauspicious and baleful influence, and Mayan rulers often planned the beginning of warfare to coincide with when Venus rose. There is evidence that the Maya also tracked the movements of Mercury, Mars and Jupiter, and possessed a zodiac of some kind. The Mayan name for the constellation Scorpio was also 'scorpion', while the name of the constellation Gemini was 'peccary'. There is evidence for other constellations being named after various beasts, but it remains unclear. The most famous Mayan astrological observatory still intact is the Caracol observatory in the ancient Mayan city of Chichen Itza in modern day Mexico.

Aztec Astrology

The Aztec calendar shares the same basic structure as the Mayan calendar, with two main cycles of 360 days and 260 days. The 260 day calendar was called Tonalpohualli by the Aztecs, and was used primarily for divinatory purposes. Like the Mayan calendar, these two cycles formed a 52 year 'century', sometimes called the Calendar Round.

ASTROLOGY, ENERGY and DESTINY

Despite popular belief, Astrology is the power of divine energy not destiny. This is the point at which most Astrologers fail when making fatalistic predictions.

The idea of Astrology being destiny doesn't just create misconceptions about Astrology, it's also a point of great struggle for the practicing Astrologer. For an Astrologer to make accurate predictions, he first must have a firm grasp of a person's Astrological blueprint. After all, if you don't truly understand the person's chart that you're studying, how can you be certain that he or she will make the choices you expect them to make? Making predictions demands a clear understanding of the person. Because predictions should come from a foundation of understanding the infinite diversity of personality and character, a 27-sign system like Greco-Roman Astrology should give more leverage to the Astrologer and the novice alike, with finer degrees of nuance than the standard 12-sign system.

But if the alignments of the planets do not create destiny, what is the actual use of Astrology? Astrology is purely energy … but this energy has a profound impact on the choices a person intends to make. To dig deeper, we will have to examine the effect of this energy. Astrological energy has two components: scientific and metaphysical. So let's examine the Moon and the Sun, the two celestial luminaries that carry the most Astronomical weight in a person's birth chart.

The Moon is one of the two most important planets in a person's birth chart. The Moon is symbolic of all that nurtures, protects, and sustains, even as it is continually changing. We refer to the natural world as Mother Nature, and indeed, the lunar cycle correlates with the menstrual cycle of women, just as it influences the tides of the oceans. The Moon is widely used in agriculture to calculate when to sow seed in the fertile earth, and when to reap its yield. Writers in antiquity often referred to the soul as feminine, and symbolized by the Moon. The earliest part of life — first in the womb, and then as a baby — also relates to the Moon, since the mother is the dominant influence during this period.

In a person's birth chart, the Moon describes the nature of the basic self, which remembers everything the conscious self forgets. Much like its role as the Earth's satellite, it symbolizes the reflection of the soul in and around the body. The Moon represents one's personality, feelings, moods, habits, memory, impressionability, imagination, and emotions. It especially represents the subconscious, which stores your karma and impressions from previous lives. Asterian Astrology helps a person become mindful of his or her subconscious, speeding up the process of self-awareness. This is ongoing process as the Moon continually fluctuates, waxing from New Moon to Full Moon, then waning down to a New Moon again. Every being on the planet is affected by this cycle.

Now let's turn from the Moon to the Sun, the other of the two most important planets in a person's birth chart.

In astrology, the Sun symbolizes the light body. The Sun is the chief of astrology, and the consistency of the Sun's alignments allow him to be the most accessible point of reference for people. Because the Sun and Moon are the most important of the astrological planets, the pair is often referred to as "the luminaries," the King and Queen of the Universe. In Greco-Roman mythology the Sun was identified with Apollo, the God of light, and Helios, the God of the Sun.

The Sun is the center of our solar system, around which the Earth and the other planets revolve, and bestows us with light and life. Astrologically, the Sun and his power allow us to shine. It is the conscious aspect of our ego, the self, and the power behind our personal expression. It is our physical life force and our capacity for leadership. It is the ethics of spirituality and wisdom. The Sun is also the power behind parenthood, especially fatherhood. The Sun also rules politics, learning, and long-lasting fame.

As human beings, we are spirits that have chosen to take form and make the absolute best of our lives. The Light of Astrology is meant to assist us in attaining our most natural selves. An Astrologer is supposed to aid people in making the proper choices that help them master themselves, rather than feeling they are at the mercy of forces beyond their control.

Outtakes from the Yavanajataka (early
translation from Greek to Sanskrit to english)

Yavana Jataka by Yavanacharya

Sage Yavana, who belonged to the Alexander period, wrote Yavana Jataka. He was an astrologer in the Greek court in India. Because of this he was called Yavanacharya or Greek Guru, and hence astrologers claim that Indians learned astrology from the Greeks! There are a few areas where his interpretations of results are different. Because of this it is an important classic. The teachings of Yavanacharya were recorded by a king called Sphujidhwaja.

Chapter 1 :The natures of the signs and planets.

11. With the twelve zodiacal signs, which are auspicious or inauspicious and which have various forms, colors, and shapes.

12. They say that this (zodiac), in which arise the seven planets, rises in a clockwise direction, and moves in strict accord with the (proper) order (of the signs) up to mid-heaven; the visible half continues on to the western (horizon).

13. . . . . (their) distinctions are established . . .

14. The first (sign) is traditionally said to have the shape of a ram; it is called by the ancients the head of Kala. Its places are the paths of goats and sheep, caves, mountains, (hideouts of) thieves, and (places there are) fire, metals, mines, and jewels.

15. The second is said to have the shape of a bull; it is the mouth and throat of the Creator. Its places are those of forests, mountains, ridges, elephants, herds of cows, and farmers.

16. The third is a couple (a woman and a man) holding a lyre and a club (respectively); it is the region of the shoulders and arms of Prajspati. Its places are those of dancers, singers, artisans, and women, and (places for) playing games, sexual intercourse, gambling, and recreation.

17. The fourth, which has the form of a crab standing in water and which is the region of the chest, is called Karki (Karkyos). To it belong meadows, wells, and sandy beaches, and its places are the pleasant play-grounds of goddesses.

18. The authorities state that the fifth is a lion on a mountain peak; it is the region of the heart of Prajapati. Its places are forests, fortresses, caves, woods, mountains, and the dwelling-places of hunters and kings.

19. A maiden standing in a boat on the waters and holding a torch in her hand is sixth, as those who are clever on the subject of time say; it is the belly of the Creator. Its lands are grassy and (suitable for) women, sexual intercourse, and crafts.

20. (The next) is a man bearing goods on a balance and standing in the market-place; it is the region of the navel, hips, and bladder. Its places are those of customs-duties, money, lyres, coins, cities, roads, caravanseries, and ripened grain.

21. The eighth has the shape of a scorpion in its hole; it is said to be the region of the penis and anus of the Lord. Its places are

caves, pits, and holes, poisonous and stony areas, prisons, and (the abodes of) ants, worms, boa-constrictors, and snakes.

22. A man carrying a bow, one whose rear half is that of a horse, (is the ninth sign); they say this is the thighs of the Maker of the world. Its places are level land, (places where there are) horses both singly and in herds, alcoholic drinks, weapon-bearers, sacrifices, chariots, and horses.

23. The tenth is pointed out as being a sea-monster (makara) whose front is like a deer's, but whose hind-end is like a fish's; they say this is the region of the knees of the Creator. Its places are rivers, forests, woods, paths and so forth, marshes, and pits.24. A pot being poured out (carried) on the shoulder of a man-this, the authorities say, is the eleventh (sign); it is the shanks. Its places are tanks, (fields of) poor grain, (haunts of) birds, and (areas suitable for) women, liquor-sellers, and gambling.

25. The last sign is a pair of fish in water; it is called by the best (authorities) the feet of Kaala. Its places are auspicious ones, (where there are) gods and BraahmaNas, pilgrimages, rivers, oceans, and clouds.

26. Thus has been told the circle of the divisions of the limbs of the Creator who made the circular surface of the earth; there is a mutual connection of the signs, marks, and qualities (indicated by the zodiacal signs) and the (corresponding) parts of the bodies of men.

27. The various kinds of places and people pertaining to (each) sign have been briefly recounted in order by the ancients; these

(various kinds) with their fixed natures are to be regarded as having their places and actions in the places and limbs connected with the(various) signs.

28. For those who are authorities say that this world of the immovable and the movable has its essence in the Sun and the Moon. (In them) are seen its coming into being and its passing away; even in the circle of the constellations does it have its essence in them.

29. The solar half (of the zodiac) begins with Magha (the first naksatra in Leo); the other half, the lunar, with Sarpa (the last naksatra in Cancer).
The Sun gives the (zodiacal) signs to the planets in order, the lunar signs (are assigned) in reverse order.

30. Others, however, state that every odd sign is solar, every even sign lunar; each solar sign is masculine and hard, each lunar sign feminine and soft.

31. In the odd signs, the first half is solar, the second lunar, they say; in the even signs, the Moon is lord of the first half, and the Sun of the second.

32. As the Sun takes Leo because of its qualities and the Moon Cancer,
so they give the remaining signs from (their own) lordships to (those of) the planets in direct and reverse order (respectively).

33. In order (these planets) are Mercury, Venus, Mars, Jupiter and Saturn. . . . Therefore they are said to be each the lord of two houses, one lunar and one solar.

34. The Horas (horai) are famous .The Drekanas (dekanoi) are renowned for their acquisition of images and forms.

35. There are portions (bhaagas) (of each sign), they say, belonging to the seven planets, and these (saptamsas) undergo modifications according to the planet. The navamsas, whose forms and actions (are taken into consideration) in genethlialogy, are (also) well known (as being useful) in making predictions, in calculating the periods of life (dashaas), and in determining the length of life.

36. In (each) sign there are dvadasamsas (dodecamoria) which fill the sign with their own influences. There are subtle modifications in respect to height or depth of action when (their) influences are combined with those of the terms (trimsamsas).

37. There are sixty solar portions (sauras) in each sign which are similar (to their signs) in what their involvement signifies. In each navamga of two hundred (minutes) there are seventy-two ciidapadas.

60. The entrance of Mars (into its exaltation) takes place in the twenty-eighth degree in the sign of its exaltation. They say that the sign opposite the exaltation and the degree having the same number (in that sign as the exaltation has in its sign) is the dejection.

61. They say that the thirty degrees in (each of) the four cardines from the ascendant are called the spikes. In every sign the navamsha belonging to that sign is named by the Greeks the vargottama ("highest in rank").

62. The mulatrikonas ("base-triplicities") of Mars, the Moon, the Sun, Mercury, Venus, Jupiter, and Saturn are, in order, Aries, Taurus, Leo, Virgo, Libra, Sagittarius, and Aquarius.

63. The human signs together with Leo and Scorpio are said by the Greeks to rise head-first; Pisces rises both ways; and the rest always rise backwards.

64. Excepting the second, sixth, eleventh, and twelfth signs from that in which it is, a planet always aspects the rest; their aspect is good when it is in good signs.

65. The influence of the aspect is complete in opposition, less by a fourth in the two "squares" (the fourth and eighth places), a half in the two trines, and a fourth in the third and tenth signs.

66. With the revolution of the three (signs in a triplicity), the groups (of signs) beginning with the first (triplicity) are said to be in the directions beginning with East in order; in these the lords of the directions are the Sun and Venus, Mars, the Moon and Saturn, and Jupiter and Mercury.

67. When the signs are without planets, one tells from their power the arrangement of the door and the directions with respect to things which are lost, have been put down, or have disappeared, and with-respect to actions, childbirth, sleeping, or sexual intercourse.

68. The measure of the rising-times of the first and last signs is demonstrated with certainty to be two muhiirtas each; know that the measure of the rising-times (of the rest of the signs) in the two halves of the zodiac, taken (respec-tively) in direct and

reverse order, is (two muhurtas) with a fifth (of that measure) added (successively to each).

69. Knowing that the signs are thus measured as being short, medium, or long, they consider the lengths of journeys as being similar to the divisions of the zodiac (and the limbs of the zodiacal man).

70. One finds that the ascendant or the sign occupied by the Moon is the body, the second place the family; the third they say is the brother, and the fourth relations.

71. The fifth place is called sons, the sixth they name the place of enemies; the seventh is the wife, and wise men say that the eighth is the place of death.

72. One establishes the ninth as the place of righteousness, and they say the tenth is work; the eleventh is the gaining of wealth, the twelfth its loss.

73. Whatever significances there are in any signs which are in the places beginning with the ascendant in order, these (significances), because of the positional, temporal, or other strengths of the signs, take on the natures of the significances in the places.

74. When the benefit planets have entered into (the places) which are called "body" and so forth, they cause these (aspects of life associated with the places) to flourish; but when the malefic planets are there or (the benefits) oppressed in bad places, they harm them.

75. Taking into consideration the good fortunes or bad fortunes of their places, which involve such things as the situations of the lords of the places and of the places themselves, the natures of the signs, and their powerful, medium, or weak aspects, one arrives at the death of men (after tracing out the rest of their lives).

76. A planet in its sign of exaltation gives a four-fold result; one in its mulatrikona half of that; one in its own house a full result; one in the house of a friend a half; one in the house of an enemy a third; and one in its dejection a fourth.

77. Planets in their enemies' houses, in the signs of their dejections, overcome (in planetary conflicts), on bad "paths", or entering into the Sun destroy the good results and increase the bad ones.

78. The semicircle from the ascendant (through the sixth place) which is to come (above the horizon), they say, is strong, that which has risen (above the horizon) is weak. The cardines are the strongest of these (places), and they state that among them the strength of the ascendant is foremost.

79. The human signs are best in the ascendant, the quadruped signs in the mid-heaven; the water signs are strong in the hypogee, the insect sign in the descendent, and the signs of two forms in the mid-heaven.

80. The human signs are strong at the beginning of the day, the quadruped and the insect signs at mid-day, Leo at the end of the day, and the water signs at night; all the signs are said to be strong in the cardines.

81. The first four signs, Sagittarius, and Capricorn are strong at night, but the experts say that the second group of four signs together with Aquarius and Pisces are diurnal.

82. Those signs-ascendant and so on-are strong which are joined with their lords, the planets whose exaltations they are, ,Jupiter, or Mercury, or which are aspected by these (planets), if they are not aspected by other planets which are in the second or eleventh place.

83. Saturn, Jupiter, and the Sun are strong in the day-time, Mars, Venus, and the Moon at night; Mercury is strong either by day or at night. The benefits are strong in the bright paksa (from new moon to full moon), the others in the dark (from full moon to new).

84. Jupiter, Mars, the Sun, and Venus are strong to the North (of the equator), Saturn and the Moon to the South, and Mercury in both. All the planets are strong in their own vargas, when they have overcome their enemies, and when they are brilliant.

38. Eighteen hundred liptakas (lepta) are equal to thirty (degrees) ; in this (matter), the distinctions according to the qualities of each are (now) to be considered.

39. The first Hora (in a sign) belongs to the lord of the sign, the second to the lord of the eleventh sign (from it). The three Drekanas in it belong in order to the lord of that sign, to the lord of the twelfth sign, and to the lord of the eleventh sign.

40. They say that the saptamsas belong to the lords of the signs (in order) beginning with the lord of the sign itself and

excluding repetitions; similarly –the dvidaiamSas are said to belong to the lords of the signs beginning with I (the lord of) the sign itself.

41. The first navamshas in (the signs) beginning with the first (Aries) are said to belong (in order) to the lords of Aries, Capricorn, Libra, and Cancer; if one counts (in groups of three) the signs beginning with (the four signs specified above, then their first) navamshas belong (in order) to the lords of (these) four signs.

42. In the odd signs, five degrees (constitute the term) of Mars, five (that) of Saturn, eight (that) of Jupiter, seven (that) of Mercury, and five (that) of Venus; in the even signs, their order is reversed.

43. The sauras, cudapadas, and liptikas are to be distributed through another zodiacal circle; each planet's portion is said to be endowed with the nature of another planet according to the sign in which it is.

44. They call (a sign) a "collection" (rasi) in order to distinguish the activi-ties of these corresponding (parts) ; this is immeasurable like the waters of the sea because of doubts as to the variety of their mutual interrelationships.

45. The (twelve) signs beginning with Aries are of three sorts, called movable, immovable, and two-natured, with four (in each group) ; at every fourth (sign) is interposed a dividing line. They are influential (respectively) at the beginning, the middle, and the end of one's life.

46. Taurus and Gemini are town signs; Capricorn, Scorpio, and Leo are forest signs; Pisces, that which travels on water (Cancer), and that which lives in the sea (Capricorn) are marsh signs.

47. The native is born with his nature affected by the changes or constancies of these signs with their natures, forms, and characteristics; if (the sign's) navamsa is in the path of a planet, then the natives feel the effect of that.

48. The ascendant, which is the first sign, they call hora (horai), the fourth from it hipaka; one also finds it called rasatala (hell), the place of water, the place of the house, and the place of increase.

49. The seventh place from the ascendant, the descendent, is called jamitra (diametros) in the language of the Greeks; the tenth from the ascendant, the mid-heaven, they say, is the mesurana (mesouranma).

50. Those who are experts in horoscopy call these (four signs) the caturlagna ("four-fold ascendant") or the lagnacatustaya ("square of the ascendant"). One finds that the place of the Moon and its square are called menyaiva among the Greeks.

51. The fourth (place) from the first they call the quartile, the eighth death; one finds that the fifth is the simple trine (trikona), the ninth the trine of the trine.

52. They say that the sixth, which gives evil, is the satkona ("sextile"), the third the dushcikya; they call the eleventh the auspicious in every way, the twelfth the place of motion.

53. They say that a caturvilagna-sign ("cardine") is a kendra (kentron), the next group panaphara (epanaphora), and the third apoklima (apoklima) this is the three-fold designation of the ascendant (and so forth).

54. Know that the ascendant, (the second, and the twelfth) (are significant) with respect to property, body, thoughts, and so forth; the fourth, (the third, and the fifth) indicate things relating to the parents and children; and the descendent, (the sixth, and the eighth) indicate things relating to the wife and to coming and going, and (are significant) with respect to injuries such as illnesses.

55. Know that the mid-heaven, (the ninth, and the eleventh) indicate things relating to sovereignty and various successes, and (are significant) with respect to the treasury and the army. Know that a cardine is made auspicious by benefit planets, even if they are weak, and inauspicious by malefic planets.

56. So in these (cardines) is bound up the mundane creation, both good and bad, with all its results; and so also in them (is bound up) the birth (of individuals).

57. They say that the third, sixth, tenth, and eleventh signs from the ascendant or from the Moon are upacaya ("increasing"), the rest apacaya ("decreasing").58. One finds that Aries, Taurus, Cancer, Libra, Pisces, Virgo, and Capricorn are the signs of exaltation of the Sun, the Moon, Jupiter, Saturn, Venus, Mercury, and Mars in that order.

59. (The exaltation) of the Sun is in the tenth degree, of the Moon in the third, and of Jupiter in the fifth; one finds (that) of

Saturn in the twentieth, of Venus in the twenty-seventh, and of Mercury in the fifteenth.

84. Jupiter, Mars, the Sun, and Venus are strong to the North (of the equator), Saturn and the Moon to the South, and Mercury in both. All the planets are strong in their own vargas, when they have overcome their enemies, and when they are brilliant.

85. They are strong in retrogression, when leaving the Sun, and when they have just risen; the masculine planets are strong at the beginnings of the places, the feminine at the end, and the neuter in the middle.

86. The Moon is strong in the first part of the night, Venus at midnight, and Mars at the end of the night; Mercury is strong in the morning, the Sun at mid-day, Saturn at the end of the day, and Jupiter always.

87. They have their greatest strength in their exaltations, are of medium strength in their mulatrikonas and houses, and have their least strength when aspected by benefit planets or when in their friends' houses.

88. Jupiter and Mercury are strong in the ascendant, the Sun and Mars in mid-heaven, Saturn in the descendent, and Venus and the Moon in the hypogee.

89. If a month is taken to begin with the first day of the bright paksha, in the first ten tithis the Moon is of medium strength, in the second it is at its greatest strength, and in the third at its least; but it is always strong if it is aspected by benefit planets.

90. The strength of a planet is established in three ways in determining about all actions-according to time, according to position, and according to strong aspects.

91. One finds strength in the ascendant when it is conjoined with or aspected by its own lord or by the lord of the exaltation which is in it, or when it is conjoined with Jupiter, Venus, and Mercury; but the ascendant has little strength in the two twilights.

92. This is said to be the method of determining the strength or weakness of the signs and planets according to the teaching of the Greeks; they say that, of the complete set of influences in horoscopy, there is an enormous number . . . .

93. Through the influence of the places and of the planets in them, which have' the greatest, medium, the least, or no strength at the times of the natives' births, men are born with the greatest, medium, or least strength.

94. The planets in the cardines exercise their influence in the first part of life, those in the succedent places in middle age, and those in the cadent places (apoklimas) in old age; (in each group) the order of precedence is determined according to their strengths.

95. At the commencement of life, one says that these are the three (groups) . . . in use; by means of these three, according to their strengths at the time of the child's birth, one finds his condition (in each period of his life).

96. If the lord of the birth, the lord of the ascendant, or Jupiter is strong and in the ascendant, it exercises its influence at the time (of one) of (the native's) four ages depending upon which of the four cardines it is in.

97. If the lord of the birth or a planet possessing its qualities and strength is in its exaltation, or in a cardine in its own varga, or in its own house not aspected by malefic planets, then it exercises its influence at the time of birth.

98. Thus they say that, of the many combinations, these are the yogas which produce complete happiness; whereas, if the planets were in their dejections or their enemies' houses, it would produce complete misery.

99. Planets in signs which rise head-first are strong at the beginnings of their periods; those in signs which rise backwards at the ends; and those in signs which rise both ways exercise their influence in the middles.

100. Those planets which are at the beginning, end, or middle of the ascendant or the sign occupied by the Moon at birth are effective with their good or bad influences at the beginning, end, or middle of their periods respectively.

101. Those navamshas which are at the boundaries of the places at birth are considered to be in them (completely); but, except for the vargottamamshas, all those at the ascendant are considered to be malefic.

102. The benefit planets, when they are in the upacaya places from the ascendant, cause the births of wealthy people; when

they are (in the upacaya places) from the Moon, they cause the births of men with many good qualities. The malefic planets, however, (in similar situations cause the births) of lepers, paupers, and men who are lazy.

103. The Moon in the cardines of the Sun produces fools, paupers, and those who are mischievous and without character; in the next (four signs) it causes the birth of wealthy men; and in the cadent signs of those who are born at the heads of their families.

104. If (two) men are born with the ascendant or a cardine of the one in the other's place, they are mutually helpful-or if they are born under signs (belonging to planets which are) mutually friendly.

105. The planets which are in the second, fourth, fifth, ninth, and twelfth places from another planet's mulatrikona are its temporary friends, as is the weak planet in its exaltation.

106. The planets which are in the first, third, sixth, seventh, eighth, tenth, and eleventh places are the temporary enemies. I shall call these the "base" (maula) friends and enemies.

107. Jupiter is the friend of the Sun, but the rest are its enemies; all except Mars are the friends of Jupiter; all except the Sun are the friends of Mercury; and all except the Sun and the Moon are the friends of Venus.

108. One finds that Venus and Mercury are the friends of Mars, Jupiter and Mercury of the Moon, and all except Mars, the Sun, and the Moon of Saturn; know that the rest are enemies, and that

the same relationships hold 4 among the men (born under the influence of the several planets).

109. Saturn, Mars, and the Sun are always malefic, Jupiter, Venus, and the Moon benefit. Mercury is benefit when it is not mixed with the other (planets) or their vargas; (when it is so mixed), it takes on a nature similar to theirs.

110. The malefic planets are hot, the benefit cold, and Mercury has a mixed nature; because of these is the result of time in the world the same with regard to things relating to generation and to decay.

111. There are said to be five great elements (mahabhutani)-earth, fire, water, air, and wind; their connections, from the body of the (cosmic) man (the zodiac), are Mercury, Mars, Venus, Jupiter, and Saturn.

112. All of the principles of existence (sattvani) are life, love, knowledge, speech, truthfulness, ignorance, and mind; they pervade respectively the Sun, Venus, Jupiter, Mercury, Mars, Saturn, and the Moon.

113. Bile is from Mars, bile and phlegm from the Sun, phlegm and wind from Jupiter and the Moon, phlegm from Venus, wind from Saturn, and wind mixed with the quality of its position from Mercury.

114. Jupiter, Mars, and the Sun are of excellence (sattva), Venus and the Moon of passion (rajas), and Saturn of ignorance (tamas); Mercury accepts the other characteristics depending on which planet it is in conjunction with.

115. Jupiter, Mars, and the Sun are masculine, Venus and the Moon femi-nine; Saturn and Mercury are neuter, their sex depending on their situations.

116. One finds that the Sun and the Moon are king, Mars a general, Mercury a prince, Jupiter and Venus advisors, and Saturn a slave. These categories apply on earth (among those under the influence of the several planets).

117. Jupiter is the caste-lord of Brahmanas, and so is Venus; Mars and the Sun are the caste-lords of Kshatriyas; Mercury and the Moon of Vaishyas; and Saturn of Sudras.

118. When the planets are victorious, so are their castes; but when they are shattered, their castes also are shattered and their qualities are co-mingled . . . .

119. The associations, acquisitions, misfortunes, and possessions (of the natives) depend upon the planets' situations; by their natures they cause (the native) to be accompanied by good friends, wealth, sons, and wives.

120. Objects are green, coppery, red, white, black, silvery, or yellow; such are the colors (respectively) of Mercury, the Sun, Mars, Venus, Saturn, the Moon, and Jupiter.

121. Father, mother, brother, wife, relative, son, and slave of the natives; such are the natures (respectively) of the Sun, the Moon, Mars, Venus, Jupiter, Mercury, and Saturn.

122. The strength, old age, activity, happiness, sexual intercourse, intelligence, and status of men are from these

planets through unalterable laws: Mars, Saturn, the Sun, Jupiter, Venus, Mercury, and the Moon.

123. The Sun is a handsome, square-limbed man, whose sparse hair is soft and curly and has loose ends. His eyes are sweet and wide in the description of Yavanesvara; his body gleams like molten gold.

124. It is his nature to be inscrutable and firm; he is a fierce, steadfast hero who is hard to assail, a powerful leader whose body-hair is yellow like purified gold and whose deeds are swift and cruel. His essence is of bone.

125. The Moon is white, shining, and handsome, with an appearance like that of smooth waters. His hair is fine and curly, his eyes wide, and his body beautiful in its symmetry; he is a youthful lover with a charming and spotless form.

126. He is wise, patient, and fond of courtesy, controlling himself in accor-dance with the laws of Manu. Speaking kindly and clothed in spotless garments, the playful Moon with pleasing eyes laughs softly and sweetly. His nature is of (the woman's) blood in sexual intercourse.

127. Venus is graceful, having pleasing eyes and broad face, eyes, cheeks, and chest. He shines like silver, his smooth, fine, black hair hanging down with curly ends.

128. His thighs, arms, belly, and shoulders are heavy and drooping; his body is made beautiful by bright-colored garments and garlands. He is given over to a love of instrumental music,

dancing, singing, beauty, sport, and sexual intercourse. His essence is semen.

129. Jupiter is yellow like ivory and gold and has a short, broad, fleshy, erect body. He speaks deeply, and his eyes and body-hair are sweet. He is pre-eminent in intelligence, memory, firmness, and resoluteness.

130. He bears authority in decisions relating to the Vedic sciences, sacrifices, sacred learning, politics, law, and the composition of poetry. Clad in white and with his hair tied up and matted, and with upright head, he is hard to assail. His essence is fat.

131. Mercury's intellect is full and pure, his body dark, his curls (as dark as) duurva-grass, and his eyes handsome. He is pre-eminent in the composition of poetry, in craftsmanship, and in the arts, and is charming because of his gracefulness, jests, and so forth.

132. He is clothed in green; he is weak, defective(?), and rotund. His speech is clear and cheerful, his body soft and of medium size. He has an unstable nature, taking on the characters of others and allowing his own to disappear. His essence is of skin.

133. Mars is a hot and passionate man with flaming curly hair and a terrible red body. The corners of his eyes are bloodshot, and he shines like blazing fire; he is powerful in his vehemence and terrifying like Kumara.

134. He is short and slender, with shining finger-nails and firm limbs. His speech is clear and pure. He is a hero, used to killing, taking, and opposing; clothed in red, he commits acts of violence and strength. His essence is of marrow.

135. Saturn has brown, inscrutable eyes. He is strong, but his limbs are curved by the bending of his head. He is tall and has thick, black, rough, and dreadful hair, and nails and teeth which are discolored and broken.

136. He is mean and very irascible; his actions are evil. Accustomed to hatred, he is a malicious master. In his black garments and looking like collyrium, thin and lazy Saturn has abandoned joy. His essence is of sinew.

137. They say that, if the planets are in the cardines in their own vargas and if they have temporal or other strength, then the natives have situations, castes, shapes, essences, and powers like theirs.

138. As these planets are strong and occupy their own dvadasamias, navamsas, and houses, they cause similar perfections of creation in the bringing forth of the limbs of men.

139. When the planets are not in their own vargas, then the signs and so forth are said to be strong, and it is by means of the natures of the vargas-according to the planets (which rule them)-that one decides upon the changes and complications (which affect the natives).

CHAPTER 2

1. Halves of the signs in the circle of (zodiacal) constellations are called by the name of their series Horas. I will describe them briefly, but in detail, together with their various shapes, insignia, distinguishing marks, and forms.

2. The first Hora in Aries wears red clothes and is flaming like the Sun at Doomsday. He holds a sword and a firebrand in his hands. His hair is tawny and sticks up, and his ear-rings are of gold. He is a fierce man who has raised the staff of Death for the sake of protection.

3. This is a man-shaped creature whose cry is loud and who has a long, thin face. Standing in the midst of flocks of goats and sheep, and mounted on a goat, he rules his host.

4. The second Hora in Aries wears a garland of skulls. His bow blazes with arrows. He has the strength of an elephant. He is bound with a half-girdle, and his clothes are black His limbs are adorned with snakes. Bearing a sword and (elephant's) skin, and of terrible figure, he wears the diadem (of Siva).

5. Entering the forest with his swift thieves, he lets loose destruction, this fearful-faced man, splitting open the highest peak with his bolts. His anxiety is destroyed and lost.

6. The first Hora in Taurus is a woman who carries a pitcher of cow's milk and clarified butter. She is pre-eminent, rising up with an axe in her hand. Her face is like that of a hone. She plays and swings gracefully, wearing bright-coloured robes, and her feet tinkle with anklets.

7. She is four-footed. Girdle-strings surround her body. She is filled with thirst, and has developed a desire for food. She is beautiful with her heavy breasts, has handsome hips, and wears a bright, pendant girdle.

8. The second Hora in Taurus is a youthful woman who is a. delight to the eyes. She is intelligent, and pale with the beauty of campaka-flowers. She knows the rules of sciences, pharmacology, and the arts. She is adorned with garments of silk, this blazing one.

9. She appears in an assembly of farmer, sacrificing her body to Brahma (?) like a woman in childbirth. She has garlands, perfumes, and cosmetic powders. Intoxicated from drinking liquors, she speaks in a lovely voice.

10. The first Hora in the third sign holds a lyre in his hand. His completion is the colour of a parrot's tail-feather. He is an artistic man with a low-hanging robe whose nature it is to love singing, dancing, and listening (to music). Seated on a cane chair he composes poetry.

11. He runs after women and is clever in love. His sides are bound in the embrace of a maiden's arms. He is not much of a businessman, but he speaks gently and sweetly, a very reprehensible person.

12. The second Hora in the third sign is established as being a woman whose actions are charming and glowing with youth. She is pale and red-limbed, clever and grateful. She is besieged by the leader of an army in a wide-spreading war. Clothed in red, she wears a long red necklace.

13. Raising her arms, she cries out when she is robbed, She is made naked by thieves in a park, but is brought back by means of an armed conflict.

14. The first Hora in the fourth sign is a woman who holds a blossoming lotus in her hand. She stands in the water, pale as the color of a campaka-flower. Her upper-garment and ornaments are pale like moon-beams. Her limbs are adorned with the splendor of full and half necklaces.

15. Leaning on the branch of an aioka-tree in a garden, she recalls to mind her beloved. She wears a golden girdle and a necklace trembles on her breast.

16. The second Hora in the fourth sign is established as being a very pale man in the middle of a garden who leans on a bright weapon and whose neck is raised (in longing). He is a lover whose radiance is made beautiful by gracefulness. Holding a lotus, the beloved one pours forth his complaints

17. He wears variegated garments and ornaments at Doomsday(?). The ointment on his body is as bright as Cupid's His allies have been destroyed, and he is remembered with the harsh words ...

18. The first Hora in Leo is to be spoken of as a bold man whose form is as terrible as a lion's, He is blazing, a fierce and hideous tyrant. He has upward-curving tusks, and is like Yama and Kala. He stands in the midst of battles between Nishadas and thieves.

19. He has bound on his quiver. Desiring to taste flavors, he slays deer in mountain caves. His teeth are like those of the lord of elephants. His firm chest is wounded.

20. The second Hora in the house of the Sun is a fierce man who delights in battle. His bow is drawn back; his garment is a deer-skin. He is a eunuch, but, bearing his amour of gold, he protects women. The hair on his body is long.

21. He is bald-headed and gat-toothed. Impassioned, he touches the genitals of a man or a woman. Together with the robbers of his band he shouts terribly and shrilly in the desert.

22. The first Hora in the sixth sign is a black and white woman who is charming and wise. She is wet with her menstruation and has filthy garments. She thinks of fine clothes, and, desiring a son, has intercourse with the man she loves.

23. She cries in the forest among the serving-girls of Brahma(?), leaning on a branch that is in full fruit and leaf. She is without wealth like one in distress, and her body is stretched out. She has attained beauty.

24. The second Hora in Virgo is said to be a man pale as moon-beams who knows how to write. He wears a beautiful and spotless garland of blossoming lotuses. He is handsome with teeth as bright as the rays of the Moon.

25. He is remembered... He adores his beloved. A pleasing man, he is eloquent and clever in crafts, dances, and the weaving of garlands, as well as in the use of a needle.

26. The first Hora in Libra is a man who is black and white. He is clever and knows spells... He carries a pair of scales, and is steadfast in the five duties.

27. Standing within the market-place, he wears bright and graceful clothes. He is in control of grain, etc., and of all sorts of coins. He carries a dart, a sword, and an arrow in his fist. He follows the vow of one who has renounced liquor.

28. The second Hora in Libra is one who is accustomed to pitiless and manly deeds. He has prominent teeth. Hating the accomplishment of protection, he carries bright-colored arrows, a knife, and a drawn sword (with which to assail his enemies).

29. He is a smasher of houses who strikes others with his fist. His hair is erect, and he is wearing a woolen cover. Crying aloud in the market-place, he jingles a bell and causes fright among the people.

30. The first Hora in the eighth sign is a man of terrible form-blazing, fierce, and most dreadful. He delights in injury, and wears a garland of gold. Yearning for battle, he dons his armor which is bound with serpents.

31. He has prominent teeth and is violent like Death. His limbs and his eyes are red, his hair like numerous swords. He slays living creatures with poison and a sword like Maheshvara angry at Doomsday.

32. The second Hora in the eighth sign is a level-standing(?) woman with a black body who has poisonous mouth and hands.

She is the cause of (the use of) weapons, battles, diseases, and dangers, as she makes her snakes swell, writhe, and sway.

33. Her neck is clung to by great serpents proud of their poisonous breath. Her girdle consists of strings of jewels. She is filled with anger, and her teeth are flashing and fearful. Biting her lower lip, she creates tumult and quarrels.

34. The first Hora in Sagittarius is a man whose bow of bone is drawn. He wears the Moon in his diadem, and is moon-faced. His hair is bound with gold. He races with his horse, this protector of the sacrifice.

35. He stands in penance in the forest of asceticism and on the peaks of mountains, slaying the race of the Dasyus. He knows the proper use of each element of the Vedas and the sacrifice, and accomplishes all his desires. His eyes are as wide as lotuses.

36. The second Hora in Sagittarius is a woman of handsome brilliance who is full of motion, pride, and playfulness, and who shims like gold. She understands magic, is artful in (the use of) poison and weapons, and gives clever advice.

37. Seated on an auspicious throne she looks at an excellent casket filled with jewels and other riches. With spotless ointment on her body as she gazes at the jewels from the sea, she shines, smiling like Lakshmi.

38. The first Hora in Capricorn is a man with jagged teeth who is hideous, and fierce, armed with a club like Death at Doomsday. He breaks the peace, this wearer of a deer-skin.

39. He guards his iron, his slaves, and his buffaloes, and, standing in the water, defends his black grain. He keeps fierce thieves who are devoted to him, Mlecchas and the chiefs of the Candalas, sending them out (on raids).

40. The second Hora in Capricorn is a woman with loose hair who has a red face and red arms and who stands on one foot; they say that the rest of her is black. Her belly hangs down, and her teeth arc dreadful like a crocodile's.

41. She shines with blue unguents, and her body is covered with a garment the color of collyrium. She is adorned with ornaments made of the metal of the Pishacas. Entering the water and standing at the Mare's Mouth (the Entrance to Hell), she raises her voice again and again.

42. The first Hora in Aquarius is a man who is as black as collyrium. His teeth are dreadful. He is black, and wears a graceful leather garment. He makes juice from the succulent sugar-cane.

43. He knows many desired arts, and his hands are employed in many crafts. A pot is on his shoulders. His thoughts are covetous; he is a friend of those whose emblem is a pot, but is not subordinate (to them). His hands hold dice for gambling. He is beloved as one who desires to defend (his friends).

44. The second Hora in Aquarius is remembered to be a woman adorned with silken garments. Her robes are black, and her hand grasps a noose. Her eyes are as wide as a lotus. She is learned in the sacred texts.

45. Her body is tall and black, her hair reddish and wild. She is by nature clever. Being in the final stage of intoxication, and surrounded by throngs of Water-Raksasis, she commands Fate together with the Night of Doom.

46. The first Hora in Pisces is an excellent lady who is loved by one who has crossed over (the ocean). Standing on a path beside the Great Sea, she is shining and moon-faced. Her laughter causes a trembling and a graceful movement of her arms and breasts.

47. Having risen up from the shore of the Great Sea and surrounded by women who are pleasing in every way, she shines forth, her limbs adorned with red garments. She accomplishes all her objectives, and is without misfortune.

48. The second Hora in Pisces is said to be a woman wearing ear-rings made of the superior metal of the Pishacas. Her body is adorned with a blue necklace and with girdle-strings having (all) the colors in the world(?).

49. Her upper-garment was made in the land of the Abhiras. She shines forth, dreadful, in blue robes. While carrying her metals in wagons and by foot, she is robbed in the woods by blazing thieves.

50. These Horas, whose purpose resides in (the determination of) the thoughts, places of origin, and qualities (of natives), are described by the Greeks by means of illustrations wherein their forms, insignia, and ornaments are successively given. They have names in accordance with their natures.

The second chapter in the Yavanajataka: the forms of the Horas.

CHAPTER 3

1. Thirty-six are the thirds of the zodiacal signs which are called Drekanas (dekanos) by the Greeks. They have various clothes, forms, and colors; I will describe them with all their qualities beginning with their characteristic signs.

2. The first Decanate in Aries is a man garbed in red and having a red complexion, a fierce man whose limbs and hands are wounded and who attacks in anger. He bears golden mail and bright arrows, and his hand is upraised with an axe.

3. The second Decanate in Aries is a pale-hued warrior whose eyes are pitiless to his enemies. He is clothed in white. His head is like an elephant's. He has arrows for weapons, and he knows the purposes of minerals and mercury. His limbs are heavy and hairy.

4. The third Decanate in Aries wears dark blue garments and has a dark blue body. Armed with a club, he is fierce. He has a blue garland of diadems. His body is exceedingly strong, and his eye-balls are like a bull's He is like the Age of Discord.

5. The first Decanate in Taurus is a black woman, winning (all) hearts by a profusion of sidelong glances. Round her neck she wears a garland full of kadamba-flowers. She shines forth holding an axe in her hand. Her body is bowed down to by cow-herds.

6. The second Dean in Taurus is a red-faced woman whose arms and lower lip are also red. She is pre-eminent as she stands on one foot holding a jar. She is always intent on eating and drinking, and delights in gardens and woods.

7. The last Decanate in Taurus is a woman with a tender body. She has a bull's hump, and wears a garland bright with campaka-flowers. Her eyebrows are fair, and her girdle hangs over the circle of her buttocks.

8. The first Decanate in the third sign carries a bow, and his hand is bright with arrows. He is adorned with a garland of many colors, and his necklace is pendant. The instruments of his craft are prepared. He knows how to use swords and missiles, and he wears a diadem and armour.

9. The second Decanate in Gemini is a black woman whose girdle is beautiful and whose garments are brightly colored. She delights in the arts, in singing, and in story-telling. Holding a lyre, she is pleased and delighted. Her brows are lovely, and she is graceful.

10. The third Decanate in Gemini wears red clothes and a red, pendant necklace. He is pale with red limbs, violent and fierce. The tip of his staff is red (with blood). He is the chief of a multitude of men. He bears a sword and missiles.

11. The first Decanate in the fourth sign is a woman whose words are beautiful and full of grace. Holding a lotus in her hand, she stands in the water. Pining with love, she is as pale and fair as a campaka-flower. She wears a single white garment.

12. The second Decanate in Cancer is a girl seated on a snake-throne, having a beautiful waist. Her heart is filled with kindness and affection. Her body, adorned with jewels, is beautiful, and her garments are of a pale hue.

13. The third Decanate in the fourth sign is set down as a woman who is the colour of a dark blue lotus and is pleasing to the eyes. Her upper-garment is of silk and (adorned with) bright jewelry. She is barren, but puffed up with pride in her beauty.

14. The first Decanate in Leo has a belly and a body like a lion's, He is fierce, armed with a sword, and arrogant with his mighty strength. His deeds are terrible and cruel, and he desires spicy food. He has many lingers (?).

15. The second Decanate in Leo is a bold woman with loose hair. She is on a mountain peak, proud in taking away the wealth of another. Terrible, she causes his death. Her actions are like those of a rogue.

16. The third Decanate in Leo is a woman whose actions are marvellous and who is cunning in respect to machines and to undertakings involving the arts, business, or jewels. Seated on an ivory throne, she considers (?) the murder of her enemies.

17. The first portion of Virgo is a black man who possesses a subtle knowledge of crafts and who knows the rules of calculating, cleverness, and story-telling. He is attached to beauty and skill, and is determined in his purpose.

18. The second Decanate in the sixth sign is a beautiful woman whose limbs are polluted by her menstruation. She loves a man

in secret for the sake of a child. She is learned; striving on behalf of her people, she journeys to a foreign country.

19. The third Decanate in Virgo is a woman who is gracefully coquettish. Her face is smiling, her countenance moon-like. Her one braid of hair is adorned with ashoka-flowers, and her steps seem to stumble with intoxication.

20. The first Decanate in Libra is a man in the market-place with the implements of his trade prepared. His limbs are covered with silk and bright ornaments; his body is black and his eyes beautiful. His places are those where there are gold, merchandise, mines, and treasure.

21. The second Decanate in Libra is a fair-waisted woman who knows meanings and crafts. She wears bright garments and a bright, pendant necklace. She is clever in the office of an intermediary (between lovers) for the sake of the bridegroom. Her actions are like those of rogues and cheats.

22. The third Decanate in Libra is a man about to attack. The tops of his teeth are far apart, and the hair on his body is long, He is wearing a heavy cover. He carries a bow and is armed with a helmet. He engages in the tricks of rogues.

23. The first Decanate in the eighth sign is a blazing man whose staff is fierce to his enemies. His sword is drawn, his armor is of gold; his flames are fanned by anger. He sports with serpents whose poison is sharp.

24. The second Decanate in Scorpio is a woman with loose hair who is bound with snakes. She is robbed by thieves in the

forest. With black body and completely naked she runs swiftly from a bandit, calling out terribly and shrilly.

25. The last Decanate in the eighth sign is a cruel man wearing a golden suit of armor. He is clever in seeking treasure in a hole. He wishes to follow a vow that is broken. He knows how to use weapons, but is tormented, having been robbed by his companions.

26. The first Decanate in Sagittarius is a man whose bow is drawn and whose speed is as violent as a horse's. He has knowledge of chariots and weapons, and bears the instruments for the sacrifice. His body is protected by gold, and his ear-rings flash with gold.

27. The second Decanate in Sagittarius is a woman who is charming, graceful, and beautiful. She is seated on an auspicious throne, and is pale with a golden-hued garment. Opening a golden casket in a heap of jewels, she takes pleasure in distributing (its contents).

28. The third Decanate in Sagittarius is a bearded man with a black body. Clothed in silk and pining with love, he is graceful. On his breast hangs a string of pearls, and a bracelet is on his upper arm. He is fond of music and perfume.

29. The first Decanate in Capricorn is the color of collyrium. His teeth are as terrible as a crocodile's, He is armed with a staff, and his actions are like those of Time and Death. He stands in the middle of a cemetery with an armour of heavy hair and a strong body.

30. The second Decanate in Capricorn is a man of blazing splendor whose teeth are dark blue and like a Pishaca's, He is handsome, having bound on his armour, sword, and helmet (shirastrana). He wanders about constructing river-embankments, tanks, and aqueducts.

31. The third Decanate in Capricorn is a woman with loose hair, a gaping mouth, and a hanging belly. Her red body is tall and thin. She holds a noose in her hand, and wears a winding-sheet. She delights in injury.

32. The first Decanate in Aquarius is a man who has dreadful teeth. He knows how to practice magic. His is the color of a dark cloud, and his hair is filthy and sticks up. His actions are pitiless. Garbed in an antelope-skin and rags, he has a vile nature.

33. The second Decanate in Aquarius is a man with a shining sword. His tawny hair stands up. Covered with garlands of skulls, he wears armor. His is the color of sunset-clouds, and his protruding teeth are fierce. He is covered with the strings of nooses and so forth.

34. The third Decanate in Aquarius is a man with various weapons wearing a garland of golden Moons. His shape is boar-like, his form frightful. Producing red (?) in Malaya, he is an ascetic whose hair is reddish-brown like a monkey's.

35. The first Decanate in Pisces is a woman with a beautiful body whose eyes are expansive and long. Her body is adorned with silk and gold. She stands by the Great Sea, which she has crossed in a boat for the sake of a heap of jewels.

36. The second Decanate in Pisces is a woman dreadful in strife, the foremost one. She is fierce, and has no clothes; her color is white, red, and black. Her garments and ornaments are destroyed; desiring clothes, she shouts out.

37. The third Decanate in Pisces is a woman whose hair has been loosened and who wears ornaments bearing the emblem of the Abhiras. She shrieks as she is frightened. She stands in the water adorned by troops of spirits having the shapes of jackals, cats, and boars.

38. These thirds of the signs which are called Drekkanas together with the natures that accompany each, to which much thought has been given, have been thus described by the great Greek masters who know the meanings, properties, and traditions of horoscopy.

39. Because of its doubtfulness, this pictorial representation is (to be) combined with (the effects of) the lords of the navamsas, the navamsas themselves, and the aspects of the planets; it is useful because it exemplifies the many forms, natures, and distinguishing marks in the world.

40. Whatever characteristics of a planet have been described with regard to the signs, the navamsas, and times, or whatever causal natures, their entire effect is in full force in all actions for whatsoever purpose.

41. What are the form, nature, quality, and distinguishing mark of (each) planet and sign has been said previously; the form which arises from the changes due to their mutual combinations in order is to be determined by a wise man.

42. They say that the form and distinguishing mark of a navamsha (are affected) by various changes because of the signs, planets, and (other) portions (of a sign); because of its situation in the rank of its own sign within a sign, they say a navamsa possesses especial strength.

The third chapter in the Yavanajataka: the forms of the Decanates.

CHAPTER 4

1. There are objects (dravyani) of various characteristics and natures which exist on earth, in the air, and in water; I shall tell of them as they pertain to the vargas and dvadashamshas (bhagas) of the signs, according to the associations (of each) in order.

2. Aries is lord of lands, fire, blood, weapons, gold, copper, minerals, smelters (agnijiva), battles, and mantras; of youths, children, fans, umbrellas, spears, flagstaffs, thieves, and commanders of armies;

3. of goats, sheep, artisans, sugar-cane (ikshuka), green onions (dudruma), mountains, (places for) assignations, and things which are burnt, cast off, or smashed; and of such objects as red arsenic (manahshila), red chalk (gairika), and red flowers.

4. Taurus is lord of games, parks, garlands, children, women, market-streets, woods, gardens, meeting-houses, and wells; of ghee (sarpis), sour milk (dadhi), milk (kshirasa), grass, flowers, city-squares, oxen, ploughs, and ploughmen;

5. of teams of oxen, yoke-pins, carts, axles, wheels, perfumes, bulls, shining buffaloes, and bulls; of works of beauty and pleasing ornaments; and of things belonging in treasure-houses.

6. To the third sign (Gemini) belong the sexual intercourse of men and women, gambling, amusements, crafts, music, singing, smiles, and instrumental music; exercise, magic weapons, writing, soldiers(?), conversations, good advice, and manuscripts (pustakani) ;

7. couples, the acquisition of money, weapons, wealth, and herbs; the bearers of knowledge, of instruction, and of commerce; those who live by cleverness, by affording humor, and by their hands; and dancers and rogues.

8. To the fourth sign (Cancer) belong women, ascetics, and Brahmanas learned in the scriptures (Sruti); rivers and white durva grass; lotuses (kumuda) and lilies (utpala); objects which are cold or soft and wet; sweets, medicines for restoring life (samjivana), and mirrors;

9. crocodiles (nakra), frogs (manduka), crabs (kulira), turtles (kurma), ashoka-trees, and water-plants and grasses; and white birds and carnivorous ones.

10. Leo is lord of peaks, forests, fortresses, poison, bones, sticks, skin, flesh, hair, deer-skins, and thread from the loom; of (animals) who live in the woods and have claws, tusks, or horns; of hunger, thirst, dry lips, flavors, and herbs;

11. of hunters, arrows, increases, and creatures who lead; of Mlecchas, swords, weapons, woolens, and gold; of diseases,

enemies, plotters, and those who are sick; and of (all) things which are strong.

12. In the sixth sign (Virgo) are virgins, sexual intercoune, love-suits. unions, bashfulness, (women) who move their buttocks(? calannitamba), liquids, smoke, and incense; materials such as ointments and rouge for face and lips, ornaments, women's playthings, mirror, and jewel-boxes;

13. lamps, ships, litters, upper garments, women's crafts, poetry, listening (to music), and beauty marks; freedom from passion(? viraga), eloquence, gems, jewels, incense, and such arts as telling stories and singing.

14. Libra is lord of such things as balances, measures, touchstones, wares, market-streets, gold, jewels, clothes, and pearls; of public criers, guides, caravan-leaders, broken, exporters(? nairyanika), and image-makers(? murtika);

15. of playboys, dice, rogues, liars, those who live by (the skill of) their hands, and those who are clever at hearing the meaning and the things to be done in message-bearing; and of the arts such as that of the six political principles (shadgunya) and that of inference, and of letters.

16. In Scorpio are holes, snakes, ants, those who are destroyed by poison, stones, or weapons, those who arc maimed or struck down, and those who are reviled; crawling creatures, scorpions (vrishcika), mongooses (babhru), and lizards (godha) ; such things as serpents and other creatures which live in holes;

17. murderers, those who are stamped on by the feet of their enemies, the corrupted, the poor, and those who obey other men's wives but wrong their own wives; flesh, stomachs, and female and male sexual organs; and vessels, implements of war, and ashes.

18. In Sagittarius are horses, elephants, chariot-wheels, bows, armour, weapons, warriors, arms, and charmed arrows; the Vedas, kindling sticks, mantras, oblations, sacrificial instruments, gods, priests (ritvij), teachers, offerings, and Brahmanas;

19. knowledge, instruction, sacred texts, those who are best in speech, poems, traditions, grammar, and auspicious materials; kingdoms, advisors (amitya), municipal councillors (puramantri), and townspeople; and Brahmanas who stand in water as well as those who stand in ant-hills.

20. In Capricorn are other animals, trees, and clove-trees; ... ; the corrupted and the ... ; crocodiles (makara) and serpents (uraga); lead (sisa), copper (loha), iron (ayasa), minerals, and nooses;

21. poor grasses (kusasya), grain (dhanya), mines, low people, slaves, causeways, rafts, forests, and rivers; those who live by ships and water; killers of deer (mrga) and birds; and whatever inhabits the waters.

22. Belonging to Aquarius are tanks, wells, dams, and obstructions; slaves, men who are terrified, and those whose bodies are spotted and branded; poor grain (kusasya), copper

(loha), iron (ayasa), and black lead (krsnasisa); outcastes (lit. "cookers of dogs"), of horses, prisoners, and old men;

23. eunuchs, ascetics (pravrajita), and those who marry low (-caste) women; cheats, bad men, and rogues; those who bark like dogs and those who howl like jackals; and pots and so forth.

24. Pertaining to Pisces arc deep waters, oceans, fords, river-banks, ships, helmsmen, (all) sorts of fish, and conchs; the sounds of women, houses, sailors (jalopajivi), baths, clothes, views, and offerings of water;

25. sacrifices, Brahmanas, ceremonies, jewels, pearls, conchs, coral, and water; ornaments; and objects relating to the Puranas, the Vedas, vows, law (niti), and righteousness (dharma).

26. Whatever the nature of a thing – be it town, dry land, forest, or water-and whatever its place-air, fire, earth, or water-a wise man may ascertain that it belongs to this or that (zodiacal) sign which is similar.

27. One must understand that objects take on various forms and characteristics due to the changes originating in the signs. Now I will recite separately each object which has a nature similar to that of each planet.

28. The Sun is lord of kings, forests, peaks, gold, copper, lions, fire, vicious animals, poisons, and woolens; and of lion-thrones, raw flesh, deserts, charred sticks, and heaps of wealth.

29. The Moon is lord of women, paintings, sleep, sexual intercourse, food, and drinks; of things which are cold, wet, or

sweet; of flavors and herbs; of garlands, garments, and land; of jewels and pearls; and of saint and lotuses (ambuja).

30. Jupiter is lord of auspiciousness, lotuses (padma), Brahmanas, gods, sacrifices, heaps of grain (dhanya), property, houses, and sons; ofgold, carriages, thrones, and nutritives; of councillors (mantri) and mahattaras.

31. Venus is lord of heaps of jewels such as diamonds, oxen, sons, women, marriages, perfumes, clothes, and ornaments; of good fortune, fragrance, listening (to music), and pavillions; of treasures and of wealthy men.

32. Mars is lord of armies, kings, robbers, the injured, and the slain; of poisons, fire, weapons, blood, and the wounded; and of gold, heaps of minerals, all sorts of flowers, and camikara-gold.

33. Mercury is lord of all sorts of merchandise, of union and separation, of cleverness, crafts, traditions, and medicine; of laughter, the interpretation of mantras, and ambiguities; and of shrines (caityas) and trees.

34. Saturn is lord of corpses, death, prisoners, battles, old men, villains, evil women, eunuchs, lazy people, and the initiated (dikshita); of those who are wretched, slavery, ointments, and cold things; and of all things which are low.

35. Each object, while pertaining to a particular sign, belongs also to a particular planet ... ; in its influence on the accomplishment of such things as actions it is to be described in accordance with the positional strength of that planet.

CHAPTER 5

1. They say that masculinity, which is the seed of the bodies of all types of beings, is solar; and that femininity, which is to be inferred to be a basis for that (seed) and is its covering, is lunar.

2. From the semen caused by the navamsha belonging to the Sun, when it has fallen in the uterus of a woman, come the bones; from the blood (of the woman) come skin, flesh, and fat and the blood is caused by the position and navamsha of the Moon.

3. The Sun, which is the father of flesh-bearing, embodied creatures, is in various states at the time of impregnation; proportionally it establishes in their bodies large, small, or medium-sized bones.

4. The Moon, because of its position and navamsha, causes the growth of skin, complexion, and flesh; and the rest of the planets with their natures arising from their portions (bhagas) and positions produce each its own qualities (in the native) in accordance with what has been said before.

5. If at the time of sexual intercourse of a man and a woman, Mars, the Sun, Venus, and the Moon are in their own vargas and are strong (lit. "brilliant"), they produce a fetus in the woman's womb.

6. In this situation, if the Sun and Venus are in benefit signs, they cause the birth of a male; but, if the Sun and the Moon are in their mūlatrikona, they produce a female foetus.

7. If these planets are in malefic, apacaya, or their enemies' signs, while the other planets are in benefit signs, then the semen is destroyed; but if Jupiter is in the ascendant, impregnation takes place.

8. If, at birth, (the planets) are in malefic signs, in injured navamsas, in their dejections, or in their enemies' houses, and are weak, pale, or harsh, they destroy the embryos or let loose a miscarriage in the womb.

9. The lords of the (ten) months (of pregnancy) are Mars, Venus, Jupiter, the Sun, the Moon, Saturn, Mercury, the ascendant, the Moon, and the Sun. The ten (stages of pregnancy) are like these planets in regard to success or failure.

10. In the first month there develops the incipient fetus (kalala), in the second there is a budding (pesi), and in the third shoots (sakhah); in the fourth bones, sinew, and the head, and in the fifth marrow and skin;

11. in the sixth blood, hair, nails, and liver; the activities of the seventh take place in the mind; in the eighth thirst, hunger, and taste, and in the ninth touch, awareness, and pleasure;

12. and in the tenth, which is the month of the Sun, the fetus, with his whole body opened up by the channels of sense, is born. Thus, in the case of all (men) beginning with Brahmanas, the time spent in the womb is divided into ten parts.

13. Those (planets) which are endowed with brilliance and strength increase the excellence and good qualities of their months; but those which are injured by malefic planets or whose

strength is broken, even though they are in benefit signs, ruin their (months).

14 . Whatever is the nature of the term in which the Sun is, such is the nature of the inner soul (of the native); his outward appearance comes from the navamsha in the ascendant or from that in which the Moon is, whichever is stronger.

15. His form is to be described from these two things, or from the Decanate in which the Moon or the Sun is, or from the planet which is strong in the configurations of the time at impregnation and birth.

16. In regard to the parts of the body, (the twelve places) beginning with the ascendant are joined with the twelve (limbs) beginning with the head; the measurement of these limbs as shortest, tallest, or medium depends on the measurement of the navamsa of the planet in that sign and of the planets' direction.

17. Planets which are malefic, in the navamsas of malefic planets, or injured by malefic planets harm these (limbs); benefic planets, if they are strong at birth and conception, cause these limbs to be splendid.

18. Malefic planets in the sixth, seventh, or eighth places from the Moon or from the ascendant harm the fetus; if the malefic planets beginning with the Sun are together in one place, they cause deterioration in the limbs.

19. Whatever is the ninth sign from the Moon as it proceeds in its course at conception, the Moon gives success to (the limb

belonging to) that sign at birth; one calculates from the navamsha in the ascendant if that is stronger.

20. If the masculine planets are together in the odd signs or masculine navamsas, or if one of their navamsas is in the ascendant, or if the vargas of the Sun and the Moon are in masculine navamshas, then (the native) is masculine because of the connection with masculine things.

21. If feminine (planets) are in the even signs or in feminine navamsas or in the ascendant, then females are born; for, if they are males, they are weak. Feminine navamsas in the ascendant beget females.

22. If Jupiter and the Sun are in vargas of the Sun and are strong, ii male is born; if Man, Venus, and the Moon are in vargas of the Moon, and the Moon is weak, they cause the birth of a female.

23. One masculine (planet), if it is in an odd sign or in a masculine navamsha, strong, in conjunction with the Moon, and aspected by a masculine planet, or in its exaltation or a cardine, gives birth to a male.

24. But even one planet in the first navamsha in an even sign, if it is strong and in its own navamsa, produces a female; or, if it is in its exaltation, it produces a female, though it may produce a male because of an excess of strength.

25. A masculine planet which is strong, is in its exaltation in the ascendant, and is under the strong aspect of a masculine planet,

is said to cause the birth of a male; a feminine planet in the same configuration produces a female.

26. If Saturn and Mercury are in their own navamsas or in cardines of the ascendant or in navamsas of the ascendant and the sign in which the Moon is or if they are aspected by them, then they produce neuters.

27. If they are in masculine places, they give birth to a neuter with a male form; if in feminine places, to one whose behavior and actions are a woman's and who is like a female.

28. If a neuter planet is in conjunction with the Moon or the ascendant or is in a navamsha aspected by neuter planets, know that (the native) is neuter and has the form of a neuter. (These configurations are effective) at conception, during pregnancy, or at birth.

29. If a navamsha of Mercury in a two-natured sign is strong and in a cardine and if a navansa of a two-natured sign is in the ascendant or the sign in which the Moon is, they say that twins are conceived.

30. If a strong planet in the ascendant aspects a two-natured sign or the navamsha of a two-natured sign, and if Mercury is in a varga of the Moon, it inevitably causes the birth of twins.

31. If Mercury is in the ascendant in the navamsha of a two-natured sign and is not aspected, it produces twins; even with respect to the rules for determining whether the native is male or female, if navamsas of two-natured signs are involved, the womb is said to contain twins.

32. If Jupiter is in a navamsha of Mercury in a two-natured sign or is strong and in conjunction with Mercury or is aspected by Mercury which is in its own navamsha then twins are born.

33. If all the planets are in the ascendant in the portions (bhagas) of a two-natured sign which belong to Mercury or are strong in their own vargas aspected by Mercury, then they say triplets are born.

34. If (the configuration at birth) is similar to that at conception and the planets are not in different positions, then the result produced by them is considered to be even greater than before.

35. The Sun is father by day, Saturn at night; the authorities say that Venus is mother by day, and the Moon is considered to be mother at night. This is always (true) – at conception, during pregnancy, and at birth.

36. One knows the characteristics belonging to the mother and father by means of such things as the good or bad places and aspects (of these planets), by means of the strength or weakness of their mutual configurations, and by means of their conditions, ages, complexions, and qualities.

37. One finds the distinguishing features of the father made clear in the odd signs, that of the mother in the even signs; the guru (of the native), with his caste and his family (jati), is to be established, night and day, from the position and configuration of Jupiter.

In the Yavanajataka: the rules relating to conception.

CHAPTER 6

1. If the Moon does not aspect the ascendant, he is not born in the presence of his father. One finds the direction toward which (his father has gone) from the nature of the signs and of the planets in order.

2. In the house (where the birth takes place) the direction of the door is to be described from the planets in the cardines according to their strength. The survival of his mother or her demise (is to be predicted) by means of the planets' being in their exaltations or dejections.

3. If the Moon or the ascendant is in a portion (bhaga) not belonging to Jupiter or is not aspected by Jupiter, they say that the native is begotten by another (than his mother's husband); or (he is begotten) by ... if a strong planet aspects.

4. If there is a planet in a cardine which is in its own house or in its own varga, (the native) is born in his own house. Otherwise he is born in a house which (is to be described) from the position of the lords of the ascendant and of the sign in which the Moon is or from their qualities;

5. or one should describe the house from the nature of the planet which is in the fourth place (the place of the house). Certainty regarding houses is obtained by means of the planets which are in their exaltations or depressions or in the fourth or seventh places, and are in immovable signs.

6. If a sign which is strong in mid-heaven is in that place, they say (the native) is born in a hidden house; if (a sign) which is

strong in the ascendant or descendent is in the same place, (he is born) in another (house); and if (a sign) which is strong in the fourth place is in that place, (he is born) in his own (house).

7. If (the ascendant) is aspected by Jupiter, (the house) is new; if by the waxing Moon, it is smeared (with cow-dung); if by the Sun, it is old; if by Mars, it is burnt; if by Venus, it is painted and new;

8. if by Mercury, they say it is a grass (hut) with many curves; and if by Saturn, it is old and dilapidated. The presence or absence of (their) qualities in the house is to be judged on the basis of the strengths of the successive signs.

9. If Jupiter is in its own portion (bhaga) in a cardine, (the native) is born in an apartment with a roof; if Mars (is thus), he is born on the ground in front of a (Vedic) fire-hut; if Mercury, he falls onto (sacred) darbha-grass or on the earth;

10. if Venus, in a lake-house or in the water; and if Saturn, in a grass hut which lets in many cold winds. If the Moon is in its own house or navamsha, (he is born) in cold water; if the Sun (is thus), in the granary of his father's house.

11. If the Moon in an even sign is either in the navamsha of a water-sign or in the fourth place (the place of water), they say that (the place of birth) is full of cold water; the same is true if Jupiter is aspected by the Moon, but it is otherwise if Mars and the Sun aspect.

12. One knows the measurements of the things pertaining to the house by means of the amounts by which the ascendant or the

Moon has advanced in its sign; one knows the furnishings, colour, and appearance (of these things) from the nature of these (i.e., the ascendant and the Moon), which depends on their positions among the signs.

13. If the Moon is aspected by or in conjunction with the malefic planets and is not waxing, it causes the loss of both mother and chid; the suffering is caused by diseases arising from the lord of the (Moon's) sign.

14. If the Moon in a navamsha of Saturn is in the ascendant, or if it is in the fourth place in a navamsha of a water-sign, or if Saturn in a cardine is in its own navamsha, and if it is not aspected by the Sun, (the native) is born in darkness.

15. If the benefit planets are strong, (the natives) listen to the sacred tradition (sruti), rejoice in good conduct, and are grateful; devoted to serving gods and Brahmanas and to righteousness (dharma), they wear pure garlands and garments and precious ornaments, and they are brilliant.

16. If the malefic planets have positional strength, (the natives) are rogues and ingrates; treacherous, cruel, greedy, and ugly, they steal others' goods; they hate good men (sadhu), and are struck by anger and ignorance.

17. If the lords of the ascendant and of the sign in which the Moon is are in their own navamsas, in their own exaltations, in their own houses, in the ascendant, in their own mulatrikonas, in upacaya signs, or in cardines, they cause the births of superior men.

18. If the lord of the ascendant is strong, it causes the birth of men having health, fame, and property; if the lord of the birth (is strong, it produces) men possessing great wealth and enjoyment, and having extensive fame and excellence.

In the Yavanajataka: the rules relating to birth.

CHAPTER 7

1. The Moon in its exaltation produces a man who is rich in savory foods, clothing, and ornaments; Jupiter in its exaltation one whose name is famous and who is honored by the king, a noble and wise man of good righteousness (dharma) ;

2. Mars in its exaltation produces a glorious man, a praiseworthy and prominent hero whom it is difficult to assail; Venus one who engages in coquetry, laughter, listening (to music), and singing, a well-dressed man who is lucky with women;

3. Mercury in its exaltation a distinguished man who speaks cleverly, a wise man who is rich in the arts; the Sun a great and very fierce man who thinks of many things; and Saturn one who obtains a command from the king.

In the Yavanajataka: the rules relating to exaltations.

4. The Moon in its mulatrikona produces a man who is wealthy because of his family and who enjoys (good things); the Sun a leader; Jupiter a mahattara, a niyukta; Mars a leader of thieves;

5. Venus a rich man who is the headman (varistha) of a city or village; Mercury one who engages in quarrels and wins; and Saturn produces a hero who is satisfied with himself and his possessions, one who is the eldest in his family.

In the Yavanajataka: the rules relating to mulatrikonas.

6. The Moon in its own house produces an intelligent and kindly man who delights in righteousness (dharma); the Sun a reddish man, intolerant and fierce, one whose actions are evil; Mercury is a wise man of charming speech;

7. Jupiter one who knows about poetry and the sacred traditions (Sruti) and whose actions are good; Mars a rich man, fierce and fickle; Venus a wealthy farmer; and Saturn a respectable man who knows no unhappiness.

In the Yavanajataka: the rules relating to their own houses.

8. The Moon in its friend's house produces one who obtains happiness from anything; the Sun a famous man whose friendships are firm; Jupiter one who is honored among good men; Mercury a man whose speech is filled with cleverness and humor;9. Mars one who jealously protects his friends' wealth; Venus a man who is dear to his friends and has a wealth of advice (for them); and Saturn a lord (of men) who eats the food of others.

In the Yavanajataka: the rules relating to the friends' houses.

10. The Moon in its dejection produces a sickly man of little merit; Mars a poor man distressed by miseries; Jupiter a filthy

man who has earned contempt; the Sun a servant who is rejected by his relatives;

11. Venus a man of no independence who has lost his wife; Mercury a stupid man who quarrels with his relations; and Saturn a pauper whose behavior is condemned and whose good character is destroyed.

In the Yavanajataka: the rules relating to dejections.

12. The Moon in its enemy's house produces a man with heart-trouble; the Sun a pauper injured by poison; Mars a deformed man whose enemies are united; Jupiter a fool and a homosexual who acts in an ignoble manner;

13 . Mercury an ignorant man who is deprived and is a slave to many; Venus one who serves a woman and has no authority; and Saturn a man whose body is tormented by griefs such as sickness.

In the Yavanajataka: the rules relating to their enemies' houses.

CHAPTER 8

1. The influence (of the planets) in the degrees of their exaltations is complete; in their navamsas, as in their mulatrikonas; in their dvadashamshas, as in their houses; and in the degrees of their dejections or of their enemies, it is the least.

2. When they are in these (places) in the vargottamamshas, they have the best influence, but of varying strength; and when they

are aspected by benefit planets, they are beneficial, attaining good fortune in accordance with the aspects.

3. One planet in its exaltation produces the results described (in the last chapter); two a man who is famous and wealthy; three the defender of a city or its governor (isvara), the general of an army who collects his own revenue, a noble man;

4. four a rich and glorious king, noble and attached to his own righteousness (dharma); five a famous and most excellent king whose treasury is increased with much wealth;

5. six a man who has inherent in him the power to acquire the wealth and strength of the king of kings, and power with respect to giving and to honour; seven planets in the signs of their exaltations produce one who is lord of the earth bounded by the seas.

6. Even one planet in the sign of its exaltation, if it is aspected by its friends which have positional or temporal or other strength, produces a king whose strength and valor are renowned and who has many friends
as his allies.

7. If two planets are in their mulatrikonas, he has a family and is a prominent leader on sea and land; if three, he has wide-spread fame and is of good family, of great wealth, and foremost in his town and tribe;

8. (if four, . . . ; if five,;)

9. if six, he is a king of good conduct and righteousness (dharma), one who has strength and courage and is the measurer of his kingdom; if seven planets are in their mulatrikonas, he is a lord of me" with the appearance, harem, and paver of a king.

10. Two planets in their own houses produce a ma" who is prominent in his family and honored by his people; three the wealthy and honored establisher of his line, a man who knows many sciences

11. four a famous and nobly dressed man who is revered hy his city, his guild, and his tribe; five the equal of those who enjoy the earth, a renowned ma", the first in his tribe, who has many pleasures, horses, and sons;

12. six a lord of men ruling his own kingdom, a man of great fame who has splendour, servants, and a treasury; seven planets in their own houses produce an emperor (rajadhiraja) the ranks of whose foes are overwhelmed.

13. If two planets are in their friends' houses, (the native) obtains his livelihood from the attachment of his friends; if three, he is a distinguished person famous for his excellent qualities who is useful to his friends and relatives;

14. if four, he is a grateful man devoted to gods, Brahmanas, and his teachers, one who is a leader in good behavior; if five, he is a wealthy and glorious servant of the king, one who protects suppliants;

15. if six planets are in their friends' houses, he has many pleasures and

hones and much beauty and he acts like a prince (parthiva); and if seven, he is a lord of men with a wealth of firm riches and with numerous elephants, horses, and servants.

16. Two planets in the signs of their dejections produce a man of base actions who is tormented by debt; three planets an unsteady character who lives in many places, a tramp and a pauper;

17. four a fool who serves others, one who has no regard for righteousness (dharma) and whose actions are invalidated by laziness; five a servant who has no house, no possessions, no wife; six a slave afflicted by calamities, fear, and weariness;

18. and seven planets in the signs of their dejections cause the birth of property-less men, low, infirm, and homeless, who follow the trades and eat the food and alms of outcastes, and who wear clothes made of air and scraps of rags.

19. Two planets in their enemies' houses cause the birth of me" who quarrel much and have tormented souls; three of those whose wealth, acquired by toil, is destroyed and who are afflicted by sorrow and suffer many losses;

20. four of those who are struck by the pain which results from the loss of what they love-their sons, their wives, and their wealth; five of those who are afflicted with the miseries and calamities of their relations and whose actions are despised;

21. six planets in their enemies' houses cause the birth of ignoble men who are pained and saddened by disease; and seven of those who have deformities and are disgusting, who are

of the lowest families and who are deprived of food and clothing.

22. These planets, in their places of influence, give results to men in accordance with their strengths; but there is also a modification of these (results) due to their being in the (various) horas and navamsas and because of their mutual aspects.

23. If a vargottamamsha is in the ascendant and its lord, in full strength, is aspected by three or more benefit planets, the Greeks proclaim the birth of kings.

24. If three or more planets are strong with directional, positional, temporal, or other strength, and are "brilliant" (vapurdhara), in cardines, and not mixed with the malefic planets, they cause the birth of monarchs.

25. If the Moon is in a navamsa of the Sun and if the benefit planets are in cardines while the malefic planets are not in conjunction with the Sun at dawn, the best (astrologer) predict the birth of kings.

26. If three or more planets in their own navamsha but not in their enemies' houses or in the signs of their dejections are at full strength and are "brilliant" (vapurudvahanti), and if they are aspected by benefit planets while the Moon is not weak, they produce kings.

27. If the Moon in its own exaltation or navamssa is in the ascendant aspected by its lord, which is very strong, and if it is full, while the malefic planets are in cadent places, then it produces a king.

28. If even one planet in its exaltation aspects the Moon in a vargottamamsha while the malefic planets are not in the cardines, it causes the birth of a king who enjoys a good realm.

29. If the full Moon is in the fourth place or in the navamsha of a water-sign and a benefit planet is in the ascendant in its own varga, and if the malefic planets are not in the cardines, then the birth of kings is announced.

30. If a navamsha of the Sun aspected by the Sun is in the ascendant, and if the full Moon is in its own house or navamsha, and if Jupiter aspected by Venus is in a cardine, then it produces the birth of monarchs.

31. If all the planets are strong and in signs which rise backwards, but not in their enemies' houses or in the signs of their dejections, and if the full Moon is in the ascendant aspected by the benefit planets, which are at their strongest, they cause the birth of a king.

32. Even one planet, if it is strong and of undiminished "brilliance", and if it is in the vargottamamsha in its own house aspected by three friendly planets, causes the birth of kings.

33. If the lord of the nativity (lit. "birth-sign") is in an upacaya place, and if a benefit planet is in a cardine or in the navamsha of the house of a benefit planet, while the malefic planets are weak, it causes the birth of a great lord of the people.

34. If the lord of the ascendant is strong in a cardine, and is in a friend's house and aspected by a friend, while an excellent

planet is rising, it produces a king who is a famous and honoured lord of the earth.

35. If the lord of the ascendant and of the Moon's sign, both in cardines, are uninjured and are aspected by benefit planets, while the ascendant and the Moon are in their navamsha, they cause the birth of lords of the earth.

36. If any planet in a cardine is in its own exaltation, house, or portion (bhaga), or in the portion (bhaga) of a friend, while the sign of its exaltation is in the ascendant, and if it is aspected by benefit planets, it causes the birth of a lord.

37. If Jupiter is in the ascendant, the lord of (that) sign (the ascendant) in the fifth house, and the lord of (the sign of) its exaltation in a cardine, and if the malefic planets, though very powerful, do not aspect, then in this yoga it produces a king, the lord of the masters of magic.

38. If the lords of the ascendant and of the sign in which the Moon is are strong, being in their friends' houses or in cardines, and if the Moon is in a water-sign or in the fourth place, they cause the birth of kings.

39. In this yoga, if the two (lords) are in the fifth place while a benefit planet is in a cardine in its own varga and a navamsha of the lord of (that) sign (the ascendant) is in the ascendant, then they produce the best king, one who is firm.

40. Seeing configurations of this sort in the horoscopes of kings, even though they have not been mentioned, (an astrologer, by

analogy), determines the influence of the planets, observing as well the good effects of time, position, and aspect.

In the Yavanajataka: the birth of kings.

CHAPTER 9

1. Benefic planets in (these) configurations always produce righteous (kings) of good behavior who are famous for their good qualities; malefic planets produce (kings) who act cruelly and fiercely, whose natures are debased, and who are unrighteous and impure.

2. If (the yoga) involves all the planets being in their exaltations to the degree while all these planets are strong, a benefit planet is in the ascendant, and the Moon is full, it produces the emperor of the three worlds.

3. If all the planets are in the vargottamas in their own houses and are brilliant (atidiptabhas) while a benefit planet is in a cardine, they produce a master of the world consisting of four continents and the sea.

4. If all the planets in their own navamsas are in their friends' houses or if, in their friends' navamsas, they are in their own houses, they produce a lord having power in their (the planets') regions in the four continents on earth.

5. If all the (benefit) planets are in benefit signs in the cardines in benefit navamshas and if the malefic planets are not "blazing" (adipta) and are not in the cardines, they cause the

birth of yogis and of munis who have the divine eye and supernatural power.

6. If, in this yoga, the benefit planets are in the cardines, and the malefic planets are "blazing" (dipta) and are also in the cardines, then there is born an honored enjoyer of the earth, whose enemies are overcome by his wisdom.

7. If all the planets, in the signs of their exaltations or in their houses, are in their own navamsas and aspect the ascendant, there is born a king of firm strength, a lord of the earth.

8. If all the planets in their own portions (bhaga) in the signs of their exaltations are strong, then there is born a learned and strong (lord) of the people, who is entrusted with the command in the world.

9. By means of the strong aspects of the signs and navamsas and by means of the aspects and conjunctions with the houses of friends, (this yoga) causes even those who originate in low families to become lords and kings, according to the positional strengths (of the planets).

10. If all the planets, being strong and to the North, aspect the ascendant, while the Moon is full, there is born a lord in the world with its four oceans.

11. If one planet is in its exaltation, the king enjoys royal prosperity on a seventh of the earth; because of the incompleteness of these (planets) (i.e., the number of the planets in their exaltations less than seven) the kings rule over a (corresponding) portion of the earth.

12. If, in the yogas or in parts of yogas, (the planets) are without strength, then (the natives) become generals (nayaka), ministers (amatya), or priests (purohita); one should describe the resulting magnitude and fortune (of the native) on the basis of the distinctions which pertain to the signs, planets, and so on.

In the Yavanajataka: the birth of kings.

13. If the Moon is in the ascendant or in an upacaya place aspected by benefic planets, it causes the birth of a lord (isvara); if the Moon is aspected by the lord of the sign in which it is when that planet is strong, it causes the birth of an overlord (adhisvara).

14. If the lord of the ascendant or a friendly planet is in the ascendant aspecting an upacaya place of the Moon, they cause the birth of chieftains of armies, cities, towns, and tribes, with modifications similar to their own (the planets') selves.

15. If the Moon in its own navamsha is aspected by Venus at night, it causes the birth of a lord (isvara) ; if it is aspected by Jupiter by day, it causes the birth of one superior to that.

16. By means of this yoga, even if it is only in a friend's navamsha, the Moon produces the best men; the Moon, if it is aspected by three friends either night or day, produces men who support their friends.

17. If the Moon is in the house of a benefit planet away from the ascendant while benefit planets are in the cardines, it causes the

birth of wise men of great wealth who have in their retinue those who have vowed to live truthfully.

In the Yavanajataka: the birth of lords (isvara).

18. If the Moon is in a house or a navamsha of a benefit planet and is aspected by three benefit planets without any other, it produces a noble man full of knowledge and science, who is foremost because of the three purities.

19. If the Moon, even though in the house of a malefic planet, is aspected in strength by Jupiter, Venus, and Mercury without being aspected by the malefic planets, it causes the birth of those who have outstanding speech and knowledge.

20. If the benefit planets are in the cardines and the malefic planets in the third, ninth, and eleventh places, the Moon in a friend's house causes the birth of wise men of good conduct; if it is waning, it produces ascetics.

21. If the benefit planets in their own vargas are in the cardines and the Moon is in the house of a benefit planet, they produce ascetics, yogis, and men of excellent qualities.

22. If the benefit planets are in navamsas and houses of the benefit planets in the cardines while the Moon is full and the navamsha of a benefit planet is in the ascendant, they cause the birth of men intent on righteousness (dharma) and sacred tradition (sruti).

In the Yavanajataka: the birth of king, of holy men (sadhu).

23. If the malefic planets are in the ascendant in the house of a malefic planet and the benefit planets are in the cardines, they cause the birth of leaders of bands of thieves whose hoards are acquired by cruel and wicked deeds.

24. If the benefit planets are in the ascendant and the malefic planets are in the cardines, they produce the strong chieftain of an army and castle; but if they (the malefic planets) are in conjunction with three benefic planets, (they produce) a firm king of wise policy and terrible strength.

25. Even one planet without the configurations mentioned (in the preceding verses), if it has temporal or other strength and is in the ascendant or is aspected by a benefic planet or is in a cardine, causes the birth of a prominent man.

26. A benefit planet aspected by malefic planets and in a bad place causes the birth of a vile, indigent, and diseased man; malefic planets give a result that is greater (i.e., worse) by a third.

27. If the Moon is in a navamsha of a malefic planet, the malefic planets are in the ascendant, and the benefit planets are weak in the houses of the malefic planets, they produce fameless men whose persons and actions are the lowest and who are censured by the world.

28. Examining configurations of this sort, from the signs, navamsas, and aspects, and from the planets, one should determine the birth and family of the vilest among men of highest, middle, or lowest rank.

29. These yogas which, because of the positions and courses of the benefit planets, have been mentioned as producing prominent men are also to be mentioned in reverse as producing wicked men when their connections are with the malefic planets.

In the Yavanajataka: the chapter on the births of kings of thieves.

CHAPTER 10

1. If a planet is in the second place from the Moon, those who understand yogas call it sunapha (sunaphi); if it is leaving the Moon, they call it anaphora (anaphora); and if (there are planets) on both sides (of the Moon), they call it daurudhura (doriphoria).

2. If these yogas with respect to the Moon do not occur and there are no planets in the cardines, this configuration, lacking the aspect of all the planets, is called kemadruma (kenodromia); it is of the lowest influence.

3. One finds that the man born under sunapha is wise and strong, of exalted conduct and independent behavior, one who has obtained fame on earth, an excellent person, bedecked and beloved, a man desiring righteousness (dharma).

4. The Moon, entering into anaphara, produces a glorious and eloquent man who is attached to business, an enjoyer whose actions are unimpaired and distinguished and who possesses all noble qualities.

5. One should know that a man born under daurudhura is a rich lord possessing distinguished enjoyments and garments, an independent man whose good conduct is well-known, a man who stands to the fore gaining fame by means of his eloquence, intelligence, courage, and other (virtues).

6. The authorities say that one born under kemadruma is a low slave to others, who does not enjoy family, wife, home, or food, one whose actions and conduct are reviled and who practices various devices.

7. The influences in the configurations called by their proper names have been recited correctly; (now) I will describe these yogas separately and in detail with reference to their connections with the planets.

8. Jupiter, entering into sunapha, produces a famous man whose intelligence is informed by many sciences, a king or one who acts like a king, a celebrated person with a family of great wealth.

9. Venus, entering into sunapha, produces a well dressed master of wife, home, fields, and quadrupeds, one who is honored by the king and endowed with good luck, beauty, position, and courage.

10. One who is born under sunapha in a configuration with Mercury is an eloquent and wise poet who knows music, singing, sacred traditions (Sruti), and sciences, a well behaved man, friendly to (all) creatures, whose fame and wealth increase.

11. One should know that a man born under sunapha of Mars is fierce and strong, often engaging in battle and thievery and devoted to riot and enmity, the destructive but rich leader of an army or tribe.

12. One should say that a man born under sunaphs of Saturn is a clever and prosperous person who is secretive in his actions, a man who is honoured or is the mahattara of a city or town, a greedy fellow of impure character but healthy body.

13. If Jupiter enters anaphara, he is a man with a family who has much wealth and does many things, a poet endowed with inscrutability, intellect, firmness, and courage, a Brihmapa or one who is handsome and of good counsel.

14. One who is born under anaphara of Venus is a handsome man who is fond of sexual intercourse and is lucky with women, a generous and affectionate person who possesses oxen, lands, gold, and merchandise, a glorious king.

15. If Mercury enters into anaphara with the Moon, he is an orator who is clever at writing and transcribing, one who is devoted to music and acts of sexual intercourse, a poet whose deeds are well known and whose knowledge is authoritative.

16. One who is born under anaphara of Mars is a proud and contemptuous leader of a band of robbers, a bold and envious thief who is eager for battle, a self-controlled and haughty man whose splendor is brilliant.

17. One who is born under anaphara of Saturn is rich in extensive lands, iron, and quadrupeds, is listened to and revered

among the tribes, and has many sons, but he is unmanly and the husband of a bad wife.

18. The Moon between Jupiter and Venus produces a master of forces whose intelligence, firmness, courage, and bravery are renowned and who has hoarded much, or the supreme head of the merchants' guilds.

19. The Moon between Jupiter and Mercury produces a clever and eloquent poet who is learned in knowledge, science, sacred traditions (sruti), and righteousness (dharma), a man who does his duty.

20. The Moon in daurudhura of Jupiter and Mars produces a man of enormous wealth whose deeds are famous, one who quarrels much, will not put up with insult, and is on his guard.

21. The Moon in daurudhura of Saturn and Jupiter produces a famous, wise, revered, happy, and glorious man, a handsome and calm person who is clever in the knowledge of stratagems (naya).

22. The Moon between Venus and Mercury produces a wealthy man who speaks sweetly, one who knows about debating, singing, and drama, and who has good food and possesses clothing and victuals.

23. The Moon between Mars and Venus produces a handsome and competent man who is lucky with other men's wives, a generous person who indulges in gymnastics, heroics, weaponry, and debates, and who desires to win.

24. The Moon between Saturn and Venus produces an honored, prosperous, and clever man who is in a position of authority, the head of his clan, but one who is a favorite in sexual intercourse with aged and sinful women.

25. If the Moon enters daurudhura of Mars and Mercury, he is a greedy and dishonest man who speaks many lies, but the chief of his tribe or a man with lots of land and money.

26. If the Moon is between Saturn and Mercury, he is a man of little knowledge who wanders in foreign countries striving for wealth, one who is honoured among other peoples but opposed by his own, a person quick to beg from others and to pay them homage.

27. If the Moon is between Saturn and Mars, he is an irate and slanderous man who has many enemies, a prattler tormented by miseries who has many acquisitions and much wealth, but whose hoard is insecure.

28. If, in these configurations, the malefic planets are in their mulatrikonas, houses, or navamsas, or in the sixth and eighth places, or in the signs of their dejections or their enemies' houses, or if they are overcome, they injure whatever is related to (that particular) sign, navamsha or portion (bhaga).

29. They say that a benefit planet whose strength is increased by its being in the sign of its exaltation or in some other place, if it is in a cardine and aspected by a benefit planet, in these configurations causes the birth of a man who is superior in the world and has great qualities.

30. If the Moon is in a yoga in one sign, it is said to have an influence equal to that of the benefit or malefic planets (it is with); whatever influence was mentioned previously for the course of the Moon is to be maintained with respect to the planets in conjunction with the Moon.

To Gain Wisdom of Asterian Astrology

O Hecate Luna,
Ego Reginum Triviarum Honoro

Repeat five hundred times on a Full
Moon

(From the CD-Queen of the Crossroads)

ABOUT JADE SOL LUNA

Jade Sol Luna in La Luz New Mexico, is the first Westerner ever to reconstruct Jyotish (Hindu Astrology) into it's original Greco-Rorman format. He became certified in Astrology from the A.F.A in Arizona, D.A Academy in India and the A.I.V.S in Santa Fe New Mexico. Luna has written for several magazines including Hinduism Today and Luna has been featured on several Radio shows across the world.

Jade Luna has traveled extensively around the planet, lecturing and conducting workshops on Astrology and Ancient Roman-Greco mysticism. Jade has traveled to India more than 30 times and spent a great deal of time with various teachers, Saints and Sadhu's in Asia.

Jade Luna consults with people privately. He usually presents a few seminars each year at various locations world wide.

During and after Luna's formal Astrological training, Bhau Kalchuri (disciple of Meher Baba) and Kal Babaji (Khajuraho India), tutored him in advanced mysticism and other forms of classical Indian lore. Jade Luna has now transformed his Indian studies into a Greco-Roman practice, showing the spiritual connection that the Ancient Mediterranean had with India.

Jade Luna is the author of Hecate: Death, Transition and Spiritual Mastery, Hecate II: The Awakening of Hydra and will be releasing a series of Astrology books in the near future. Jade has been one of the most successful Astrologers in the world and has maintained a high level practice for over 16 years.

Special thanks to Gianna for the great help with this book. My mother for her interest in Astrology, my brother Sky for his strength, my Dad for his love of nature. To Roye and the Anastasio's, Richard Bourke, Bija Bennette. Wendy and Gary Broad, Solar Culture Gallery, Santa Fe Soul, Healing Essence and to my long time clients who opened the door to the success of my work.

Available everywhere

CD-Scorpio Invocatio

The Third CD release from the team of Jade Luna and Jordan James on Legatus Records. This is a strong meditative chant that takes the listener deep into the constellation Scorpio, the home of the Greek Goddess Hecate. Deep droning undertones create a soundscape of intensity and transformation. Not your typical meditative CD, but something very real and original. A must for those that want to explore the deep subconscious.

CD-Zodiac Hymns

Another Jade Luna and Jordan James collection of Ambient chanting Cd's on Legatus Records. This CD is Pre-Augustus Latin Chanting to the Planetary Gods. It is an Ambient CD mixed with Egyptian and Greek undertones. Awesome for meditations that take you back to Ancient Rome and Greece.

CD-Queen of the Crossroads

Ambient at it's finest. Deep, beautiful but haunting soundscapes mixed in with lovely Latin chanting from Jana. This chant was specifically designed to invoke the form of the Mother Goddess "Hecate Luna", for the gift of divine intuition. The dark intonations deal with moving the listener past the subconscious fears that stop real intiuition. A must for psychics,Hindus, Wiccans, mystics, those trying to develope intuition, or any worshipper of the Divine Mother.

Roman/Greaco information from "Gods of the Greeks", Homerica and OVID

Star Symbols from Sirius Software-
WWW.ASTROSOFTWARE.COM

References:

Roman/Greaco Astrologers:

Alexander Volguine (thank you for preserving as much as possible of the Ancient Lunar Greek System)
Paulus Alexandrinus
Ptolemy
Lucius Taruntius Firmanus
Theophilus of Edessa
Rhetorius
Marcus Manilius
Julius Firmicus
Nigidius Figulus

Vedic Astrologers:

Laura Barat
K.S. Krishnamurti (who was "intuitively" an inch away from recreating the ancient Greek system)
B.V. Raman
James Braha
The Astrologers at "Dirah Academy International" who helped enormously with the "Star" section of this book

David Frawley (brilliant being)
V K Choudhry and K Rajesh Chaudhary
Chakrapani Ullal
Ancient Western Astrology references:
BIBLIOGRAFIA DE LA HISTORIA DE LA ASTROLOGÍA
GRECORROMANA - Universidad de Málaga. Comprehensive
list of secondary material -- strong on journal articles.

CUMONT ASTROLOGY LIBRARY AT ACADEMIA
BELGICA - Dedicated to scholar Franz Cumont (one of the
editors of the CCAG and early scholar in Mithraism, Hellenistic
religion and astrology). Contains bibliography of works on the
history of astrology.

GARY THOMPSON'S BIBLIOGRAPHY OF ANCIENT
ASTRONOMY - Excellent resource that covers Babylonian,
Egyptian, Greek and Arabic astronomy (especially concerning
the constellations and star names).

HISTOIRE DE L'ASTROLOGIE OCCIDENTALE
BIBLIOGRAPHIE - Ancient astrology bibliography by David
Juste. Excellent list!

STAR OF BETHLEHEM BIBLIOGRAPHY - Bibliography
containing journal articles, books and web resources on all of
the theories about the astronomical basis to the Star of
Bethlehem. Listing contains general resources on hellenistic
astrology, as well.

BIBLIOGRAPHY OF ISLAMIC ASTRONOMY - Extensive
Bibliography of Astronomy and Astrology in Baghdad in the
9th and 10th centuries.

Online Texts and Translations
TRANSLATION TEXT OF 'ANONYMOUS OF 379' -
Anonymous of 379 A.D. is a Late Empire Greek writing
astrologer who delineates fixed stars, comets and other
phenomena. This is an English translation by Daria Dudziak.

ONLINE TEXT (LATIN) OF MANILIUS - Manilius was a 1st
Century C.E. Latin writing astrologer who authored a long
cosmological poem. Compared to other writers of the time, his
astrological material differs quite a bit from the Greek writing
(Hellenistic) astrologers.

TRANSLATION OF RHETORIUS (ITALIAN) -
INSTRUCTIONS ON JUDGEMENT OF THE NATIVITY -
Rhetorius is considered the last of the late Hellenistic
astrologers. He flourished in the early 6th century and preserves
sections by earlier astrologers such as Teukron of Babylon and
Antiochus of Athens. Ninety chapters of his large compendium
survive and are available throughout the volumes of the CCAG.
Translated by Guiseppe Bezza.

TRANSLATION OF RHETORIUS (ITALIAN) - ON THE
NATURE AND VIRTUE OF THE PLANETS - From the same
site. Also translated by Giuseppe Bezza.

SCANNED MANUSCRIPT (LATIN) OF ALCABITIUS -
Medieval astrologer Abd-al-Aziz Ibn-Utman al-Qabisi. Alcabitii
Ad Magisterivm iudiciorum astrorum Isagoge. Commentario
Ioannis Saxonij declarata.

Brief Histories and Surveys

BREVE GUIA DE HISTÓRIA DA ASTROLOGIA NO OCIDENTE - Brief History of Western Astrology by Brazilian astrology Barbara Abramo (in Portuguese).

CIELO ET TERRA - associazione per lo studio dell'astrologia classica - Association for the Study of Classical Astrology. Italian site with some English translation.

VETTIUS VALENS AND PTOLEMY - Website of Professor Mark Riley. Scroll to 'scholarship' section for PDF's including a survey of Valens and journal articles on Claudius Ptolemy. (These PDF's have a long download time.)

DOROTHEUS OF SIDON - Brief article on Dorotheus of Sidon by Nick Campion.

Related Ancient Astronomy/Astrology Links
C.U.R.A. ASTROLOGY RESEARCH JOURNAL - Articles on ancient and modern astrology in French, English, and Spanish.

SECRET CHAMBERS OF THE SANCTUARY OF THOTH - Articles by Joanne Conman on the Egyptian astronomy and religion, including an analysis of the Dendera Zodiac ceiling.

JOURNAL OF MITHRAIC STUDIES - This ancient and mysterious Roman religion involved some level of Hellenistic astrology, though the question of to what extent and what it means is hotly debated. Some issues available on the web, though the file size for each page is enormous.

RENAISSANCE ASTROLOGY - This site of practicing astrologer, Christopher Warnock, Esq., contains biographies on astrologers and related figures of the Renaissance, as well as information on Renaissance practice of astrological magic.

THE NERO PREDICTION - An astrological novel by Humphry Knipe which centers around a reconstruction of Nero's life based on his horoscope and the Roman/Hellenistic methods of interpretation.

Jyotish References:

The Yavanajataka of Sphudjidhvaja, 2 Vols., ed., tr., and comm. by David Pingree (Cambridge, MA and London: Harvard University Press, 1978).

Brihat Parashara Hora Shastra -Translated by R. Santhanam

Brihat Jataka (one volume with extensive and interesting notes by the translator) and Sri Sarwathachintamani (two volume set with extensive, useful commentary of this major Vedic classic)- both translated by B. Suryanarain Rao

Jataka Parijata (3 Vol) (/w Original Slokas in Sanskrit and English Trans. My Vedic teacher, Hart often quotes this important work that is used as the textbook in Vedic studies in India) by Subramanyam Shastri

Kalaprakasika - ranslated by N.P. Subramaria Iyer

NOTES:

TARA INTERNATIONAL

INDIA RESEARCH PRESS / TARA PRESS INTERNATIONAL

INDIA

Corporate Office -
B-4/22,Khajuraho - 110 029, INDIA
Telephone : 91-11-2369 4610 Telefax : 91-11-2471 8637

Editorial Office -

Flat #6, TRUST OFFICE - 110003, India.
Tel: 00.91.11.2469 4610, 2469 4855
TeleFAX: 00.91.11.24618637, 417 57 113

AMERICA

JSL INC Press.
14431 Ventura Blvd suite 538
Sherman Oaks CA 91423

WWW.ASTERIANASTROLOGY.COM
WWW.ATROLOGYSPHERE.COM